Arnold House School

OUR HISTORY, OUR HOUSE

Arnold House School

OUR HISTORY, OUR HOUSE

NIGEL WATSON

THIRD MILLENNIUM
PUBLISHING, LONDON

© Arnold House School and
Third Millennium Publishing Limited

First published in 2013 by
Third Millennium Publishing Limited,
a subsidiary of Third Millennium
Information Limited

2–5 Benjamin Street
London
United Kingdom
EC1M 5QL
www.tmiltd.com

ISBN 978 1 906507 95 4

British Library Cataloguing in Publication Data
A CIP catalogue record for this book is available
from the British Library.

Managing Editors: Susan Millership and
Stephanie Miller
Designer: Helen Swansbourne
Production: Bonnie Murray
Reprographics by Studio Fasoli, Italy
Printed by Gorenjski Tisk, Slovenia

Front and back cover photography
© Nicky Colton-Milne

With thanks to Katerina Maidment for her
inspiration in the naming of this book.

Contents

Acknowledgements

Arnold House is a happy and welcoming place. That is largely thanks to Viv Thomas and his colleagues. I would particularly like to thank Stephanie Miller and Richard Fletcher for their hospitality, help and advice. I am also grateful to those members of the catering staff who regularly mounted the stairs to the top of the School to keep me and my interviewees fed and watered. With such large gaps in the documentary coverage of the School's history, this book would have been very thin indeed without the willing cooperation of all the people I interviewed. It was a pleasure meeting them all and they showed me that the true value of the School lies in the happy atmosphere it has sustained and the lifelong friendships that have resulted. In this regard I would like to thank – Nicholas Allen, Annabel Batty, Peter Beckman, Edward Brett, David Burr, Gilly Clegg, Andrew Cuthbertson, Susie Dart, Anastassis Fafalios, Charles Falk, William Falk, Nick Fear, John Fingleton, Freddie Fox, Terry Grimes, Edward Grouse, Daniel Hahn, John Hill, Nicky Huish, Chere Hunter, James Hyman, Graham Jacobs, Leonard Jacobs, Antony Japhet, Peter Kemp, Hugo Langrish, George Lester, Alan Lipscomb, Rick Martin, Jonathan Naggar, Tim Piper, John Prosser, Gerald Raingold, Howard Raingold, Lesley Ralphs, Peter Rawlins, Tony Roques, Colin St Johnston, Ed Sanders, Viv Thomas, John Ungley, Eddie Villiers, Alan Warner, Penny Williams, Colin Winser, Carlyn and Jon Zehner. I would also like to thank Fiona Daniels, whose husband was a descendant of the Hanson family, for the fascinating additional information she kindly shared with me about Amy Hanson. My very first commission, many years ago now, was for a boys' prep school; it has been a pleasure to return to a prep school after so long. I have enjoyed attempting to capture the spirit of Arnold House. Needless to say, any errors that remain may be attributed to me.

NIGEL WATSON
Summer 2013

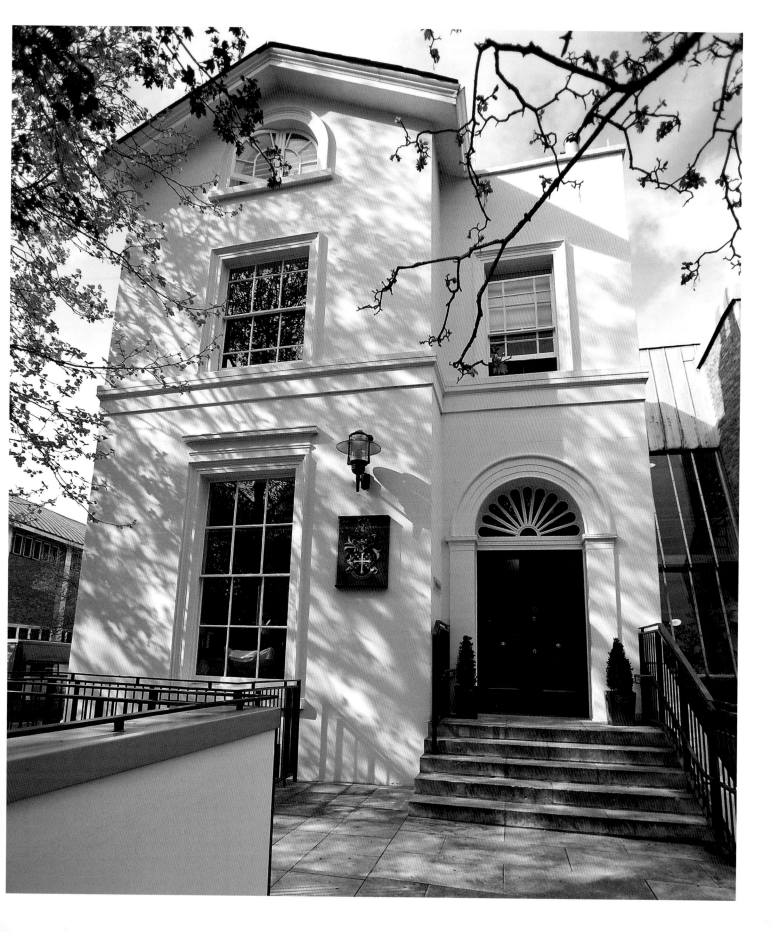

Foreword

The year 1905, midway through the Edwardian era when Miss Hanson opened Arnold House with nine boys, is a world away from today. She clearly had a vision when she chose to name her new school after Thomas Arnold, the revered educationalist, historian and former Headmaster of Rugby School; a vision that was rooted in giving young boys the very best environment in which to develop into self-reliant young men of good character, whatever abilities they possessed.

The novelist L.P. Hartley famously wrote, 'The past is another country; they do things differently there', but in the case of Arnold House, Miss Hanson would be just as proud of the boys and staff today in 2013 as she was when she led the School herself. For all of us who have had the good fortune to be touched by Arnold House at some point in its history there is no doubting that it has instilled in us a sense of pride and affection. In short, this is a school with a great heart.

The governors and I are indebted to the author, Nigel Watson, whose craftsmanship has enabled the story on the page to flow and to Stephanie Miller, our Director of Development, whose keen eye for detail has contributed so much to the vibrancy of the narrative. *Our History, Our House* is for all those who have been associated with the School, whether a pupil, member of staff, parent or friend. I hope you enjoy reading it as much as I have.

VIV THOMAS
Headmaster

Arnold House School.
51 Wellington Road.
St Johns Wood. N.W.

School opened Monday Se[p]
Class List

Seniors.
Ritchie
Benjamin
White
Vignoles I
Eachy.

Examination Results.

Latin. 1st Ritchie 95/100 Arith: 1st Benjamin 88
French 1st Vignoles I 45/50 Writing 1st Vigno
Geog. 1st. Ritchie. History 1st. Eachy & Be
Top of Form I. Prize Giving Jun
Prizes given away by Canon Duck
Ticket prizes gained by [Ritchie] Vignot
Benjamin. French Prize, Vignoles II.

'A High Class Preparatory School for Little Boys'
1905-18

Amy Hanson's diaries

Perhaps the most precious part of the archive belonging to Arnold House School are a number of large bound manuscript books. Stuffed with so many press cuttings and other memorabilia, they are bulging and bowed. The work of many different hands, the first is prefaced by the inscription, 'Arnold House School, 51 Wellington Road, St John's Wood, NW'. The first entry notes simply, 'School opened Monday September 25th 1905.' The class lists feature the names of just nine boys – Benjamin, Eady, Richie, Vignoles I and White in the senior list, and Baker, Borradaile, Delmar-Williamson and Vignoles II in the junior list.

A few weeks earlier a circular had been issued under the names of the two Headmistresses of the new school. Miss Hanson and Miss Hughes, it announced, in response to many requests from local parents, were opening a 'High Class Preparatory School for Little Boys'. The notice set out the credentials of the two women. Miss Hanson was registered by the Board of Education and had been senior assistant mistress of the prep school

Left: The School,
Summer 1905

Below: The 1905
prospectus

run by Miss Woodman and Mr Egerton at 13 Somerset Street nearby. Miss Hughes held qualifications from Queen's College in Harley Street, opened in 1848 specifically for training women teachers, as well as the Higher Cambridge Certificate, and had taught at Somerset Street and another prep school, The Briary, in Westgate-on-Sea. Boys, it said, would benefit from the individual attention derived from small classes. Miss Hughes would also teach a special class preparing boys for the entrance examination to the Royal Navy. Fees would start at ten guineas a term. Based on the rise in average earnings since 1905, this would be the equivalent in 2012 of £3,450.

We know little about Miss Hughes, who had obviously taught alongside Miss Hanson at the prep school in Somerset Street. Perhaps it was there that the two women first discussed the idea of setting up their own school. Miss Hanson's early years too are shadowy. The eldest of five children, Amy Hanson was born in Pershore, Worcestershire, in 1871. Her father Peter was a draper, whose deep involvement in the town's affairs earned him widespread affection. She was devoted to him, looked after him in his final illness, paid for the family memorial in the local cemetery and donated a glass cabinet in his memory to Pershore Abbey. While he left his estate divided equally among his surviving children, he seems not to have taken in the undoubted achievement of his eldest child in building

PREPARATORY SCHOOL FOR BOYS,

ARNOLD HOUSE,
51, WELLINGTON ROAD, N.W.
(Near Lord's Cricket Ground).

Miss Hanson and Miss Hughes, assisted by a staff of Tutors and Mistresses, prepare boys between 5 and 13 years of age for the Preparatory Boarding, and Public Schools, and the Royal Navy. They have both made a special study of the education of young boys, are highly qualified, and have had great experience in Preparatory School work.

Miss HANSON (registered by the Board of Education) has been for many years Head Assistant-Mistress at 13, Somerset Street Preparatory School, under both Mrs. Davenport (Miss Woodman) and Mr. George Egerton.

Miss HUGHES (Certificate Higher Camb. Maths., Literature, Mental and Moral Science, Maths. Certs: Queen's College, London, Member Math. Assoc.) was Mathematical Mistress at Mr. Napier Kingdon's Preparatory School, Westgate-on-Sea, formerly Mathematical Mistress at 13, Somerset Street.

Position.—The House is detached, and has been adapted expressly for School purposes The rooms are large, cheerful, and exceptionally well ventilated. The School is about ten minutes' walk from Regent's Park. There is a good sized playground attached to the house, and an indoor play-room and carpenter's shop. The drainage and sanitary arrangements are all new, and have been modelled on the latest and most approved methods—and the house and premises are inspected every term.

Work.—The boys are thoroughly grounded, and the education is carried out on the most modern lines. The subjects taught include English, Latin, Greek, French, Arithmetic, Algebra, Geometry, Nature Study, Pencil and Brush Drawing, Musical Drill, Class Singing, and Elementary Science (illustrated by Lantern Lectures). In the case of the little boys great importance is attached to the English Subjects and care is taken to give them as much variety as possible. Reading, Writing, Spelling and Arithmetic (daily lessons), Elocution, Geography, History, &c., are all taken in turn. All boys are taught Drawing on the Ablett System, and are encouraged to make original sketches and illustrations. Every boy is expected to take up some branch of Natural Science.

A Short Bible Lesson is given every day.

Amy Hanson, 1916

up one of the capital's most respected prep schools, referring in an interview given shortly before his death to his sons but mentioning of his daughters only their marriages.

Before Amy came to London, she taught as an assistant mistress at a small school in Ilkley in the West Riding of Yorkshire. Teaching was one of the few occupations open to unmarried young middle-class women at the time. Educational opportunities for women were improving but remained limited. When Queen's College, which Miss Hughes attended, was opened in 1848, catering exclusively for the education of young women, it was regarded as socially subversive. Amy may have been educated at one of the new elementary schools created by the Education Act of 1870 rather than being educated at home, and could possibly have attended the new school for girls established in nearby Worcester in 1883. The first university to admit women to degrees was London in 1878, followed by a steady trickle of others, although Oxford and Cambridge held out until well into the 20th century. There was a limited choice for women seeking a profession. Both branches of the law remained closed to women until after the First World War. There were just 264 women registered as doctors by 1895 and only a handful who had qualified as engineers. Together teaching and nursing employed more educated women than all the other professions. Women who chose teaching had limited opportu-

nities for training. The first women-only teacher-training college, Whitelands, opened in 1841 but the number of students remained small. In 1878 Whitelands was the largest training college in the country, with 140 students. By then Whitelands and other colleges were training women for the new elementary schools. In contrast, the Froebel Society, formed in 1874, and the National Froebel Union, founded in 1887, which expounded the child-centred educational philosophy of Friedrich Froebel, were directed more at the management of small groups of children in private schools. Judging from the absence of any information in the 1905 circular, Amy Hanson probably learned everything she knew about teaching from experience.

The idea of the two women to establish their own school for young boys was a brave one, even if it was not unusual. A number of similar schools flourished in the late 19th century, often run by spinster sisters or, as with Misses Hanson and Hughes, as a partnership. Most of the educational establishments found in St John's Wood in the mid-19th century were run by women. It was not easy. The classics were still the core of the preparatory school curriculum yet few women received any classical training – a deficiency they overcame usually by recruiting qualified male teachers. Miss Hanson was the exception; the printed Arnold House staff list in 1908 shows she taught classics as well as geography.

The Association of Headmasters of Preparatory Schools (AHPS) was founded in 1892 specifically to cement the relationship between the public and preparatory schools. By 1900 it was reckoned there were more than 400 boys' prep schools. A survey of AHPS schools by the Board of Education in 1900 revealed most of them were boarding schools, with just 17 predominantly day schools among the 54 schools admitting day boys. They ranged in size from fewer than 20 boys to more than 70, although just six schools exceeded the latter figure. Most boys entered at nine and left at 13. Forms were small,

Preparatory schools for boys

The boys' preparatory school was well established by the time Arnold House opened. Private schools had been educating young boys for places at the public schools since the early 19th century. The relationship between the two became closer following the Clarendon Report of 1864. This was one of several reports that fostered educational change during the second half of the 19th century. The report specifically categorised as prep schools those institutions supplying most boys to public schools. Clarendon's recommendation that all younger boys should be educated separately from older boys was the spur for the further development of prep schools. This changed the age of entry to the public schools and led to the founding of more prep schools during the 1860s and 1870s. It brought the two sides closer by linking them through entrance examinations and scholarships, with the latter acting as a particular stimulus to the growth of prep schools in the second half of the century. Many public schools increased the number of scholarships they offered. At Westminster, for example, the number rose from three to 11 between 1889 and 1899. Most boys still entered public school by entrance examination and strong links developed between particular public schools and prep schools. Many preparatory schools were also educating boys for entry at 13 into the Royal Navy through the Royal Naval Colleges at Osborne and Dartmouth, a system only abolished in 1948.

Cadets in Drill Dress, Osborne College.

Royal Naval College, Osborne

with eight or nine boys in each, and the facilities were varied. The most well-equipped schools might boast a covered gym, carpenter's shop, detached sanatorium and extensive gardens. Many were squeezed into converted villas with narrow staircases, small classrooms and limited grounds.

Most prep schools were run by men, the majority of whom were Oxbridge graduates. Typical was a nearby neighbour of Arnold House, Loudoun House School in Loudoun Road. It was established in 1888 by Stephen Cox Newton, who had won his cricket blue at Cambridge in 1876 and played first-class cricket until 1890. He was captain of Somerset from 1880 until 1884, during which time it became officially recognised as a first-class side, and he also appeared for Middlesex in 1885. The school, housed in a converted villa, admitted both day boys and boarders. When Luigi Denza joined Loudoun House,

as a young boy, in 1899, there were 80 boys in six forms. Like many other prep schools, Loudoun House offered a classical curriculum but little in the way of art or music. Denza recalled playing football on an asphalt pitch at the rear of the school and catching the train to Wembley or taking a long walk up Fitzjohn's Avenue to Hampstead Heath to play cricket during the summer.

For Amy Hanson and her friend to compete in this predominantly male-led environment was not something to be undertaken lightly. Miss Hanson would later recount how she would occasionally borrow a horse and carriage from a local doctor with whom she was friendly so she could be seen driving around the neighbourhood. It was only in the early 1970s that the AHPS's successor, the Independent Association of Prep Schools (IAPS), finally admitted schools led by women.

Right: Thomas Arnold

Below: Loudoun House School in 1910. Arnold House moved here in 1914

But Miss Hanson and Miss Hughes judged their catchment area well. St John's Wood was leafy and prosperous, populated by the comfortably off upper middle classes who were ambitious for their young sons. It was a cosmopolitan district, the home of European exiles, of intellectuals and academics, artists and musicians, journalists and writers (Luigi Denza's Italian father was a composer of drawing-room ballads, as indeed was the father of Delmar-Williamson at Arnold House). There were several Arnold House schools up and down the country but naming the new school after Thomas Arnold, Rugby School's illustrious educationist and intellectual, was an apposite choice for the district.

It was also perhaps easier for the two principals to make a start because the Common Examination for Entrance to Public Schools had replaced individual entrance examinations in 1903. There was no immediate urgency to establish close relationships with any one public school as had often been the case in previous years. While Greek and Latin were foremost among the subjects examined, the position of the classics in the prep-school curriculum was under threat, and by 1909 Greek had been omitted, with greater emphasis on English. This too helped to ease the early years of Arnold House.

Amy Hanson also knew the value of promoting the School and cultivating relationships with the prosperous and influential in the neighbourhood. On 14 July 1906, when the School held its first Sports Day, the prizes were presented by Lady Robert Cecil, whose husband, later one of the architects of the League of Nations and winner of the Nobel Peace Prize in 1937, had just been elected as the local member of parliament. Distinguished guests graced Prize Giving, such as the Colombian ambassador, Señor Pérez Triana, in 1913. The two women must have had persuasive charms as shown in the list printed in 1908 of past and present parents happy to provide a reference on behalf of the School. Among a number of medical men resident in Upper Wimpole Street and Harley Street, one of the most prominent was Sir Dyce Duckworth, who had been physician to Edward VII as Prince of Wales. Another referee was Arthur Rackham, living in Primrose Hill, already well-known as one of the country's leading illustrators. The list included a heavy sprinkling of titles, such as the Marchioness of Bath, the Viscountess Parker and the Lady Florence Grant. Several came from distant parts and clearly sent their sons as boarders. The family home of Lady Victoria Dawnay was stately Beningbrough Hall near York, now owned by the National Trust, while Mrs

Charles Leveson-Gower resided at Titsey Place, near Oxted, one of Surrey's largest surviving historic estates. The joint Headmistresses were also eager for official recognition. In 1908 they applied to the Board of Education to be recognised as an efficient school and invited an inspection to be arranged, failing to appreciate that the regulations governing

Left: Sir Dyce Duckworth

Above: Arthur Rackham

Below: Letter regarding the dissolution of the partnership, 1910

ARNOLD HOUSE SCHOOL.
18th November, 1910.

Dear Sir or Madam,

We beg to inform you that the partnership between us has been dissolved, and the School as from the 17th September last has been acquired by Miss Hanson, who will henceforth carry it on alone. We hope you will continue to extend your favour to the School on this change.

Miss Hughes (Now Mrs. J.W. Clouston) has, with Mr. J.W. Clouston, started a preparatory school for boys in the country at Semer House, Semer, near Ipswich.

When the parents or friends of any boys at Arnold House are contemplating their removal in order to send them away from home, we hope they will give their favourable consideration to Semer House.

Yours faithfully,

A.M. HANSON.

K.E.A. CLOUSTON.

Wellington Road

Fifty-one, Wellington Road, the School's first home, has long since been replaced by a nondescript block of flats but early photographs show a road of large, elegant detached houses converted from residential use. In an age when epidemics were frequent in schools, and child mortality rates were high, the School emphasised its attention to health and hygiene. The rooms were 'exceptionally well-ventilated' and 'the drainage and sanitary arrangements ... all new', adding that the drains were 'thoroughly cleansed, tested and certified before the beginning of each term'.

Wellington Road, early 1900s

inspections did not then apply to prep schools. Miss Hanson also made sure that she was available to parents, who were invited to see her without an appointment for an hour each morning every Monday to Wednesday. She would also host social evenings, 'At Homes', during the summer. As a result, from those first nine boys in 1905, numbers rose gently to reach 48 in 1909. In the following year marriage claimed Miss Hughes. She fell for a member of staff and became Mrs Clouston in September 1910, moving with her husband to set up a boys' prep school at Semer House, Semer, near Ipswich. This school appears to have been relocated several times before settling at Brickendonbury in Hertfordshire until Mr Clouston's retirement in 1939. It seems also to have survived after the war, but for how long is unknown. With the marriage of Miss Hughes, Miss Hanson took sole charge of Arnold House.

There were a dozen full-time and part-time staff in 1908. Miss Hanson emphasised that she was assisted by teachers who were 'Oxford and Cambridge graduates and trained and highly qualified mistresses'. There were five female classroom teachers, including Mademoiselle Della Santa, who taught French. The curriculum covered Latin, Greek, English, French, arithmetic, algebra, geometry,

nature study (which included 'reproduction') and drawing. Elementary science was illustrated by lantern lectures. A short Bible lesson was given each day. For the junior boys, the emphasis was on reading, writing, spelling, arithmetic, elocution, geography and history. Miss Hanson insisted that the main aim of the School was 'the training of character', adding that 'the school system seeks to foster a sense of honour and a spirit of self-reliance'. But within the classroom she stressed that the School sought 'to develop to the full, without pressure, whatever abilities a boy possesses – to encourage him to do his best – and to cultivate a love of books and work for their own sake'. Arnold House has followed this philosophy consistently ever since. To back this up, boys who had been absent or were having difficulties with their lessons were given special attention, 'so that neither the boys nor their class may suffer'. Even then middle-class parents most ambitious for their sons to succeed were employing private tutors, some of whom would eventually establish their own schools. Miss Hanson was obviously aware that this practice went on but then, as now, there was little that could be done to stop it. Instead, she tried to give parents an alternative, offering to arrange 'special coaching for higher maths, classics and modern languages for

Swedish Drill and
programme, 1916

scholarships etc'. Scholarships were understandably highly prized by Miss Hanson. One of the first went to J. da Costa Andrade, one of the first Jewish boys to enter the School, who won a scholarship to Charterhouse in 1912.

Physical recreation was the preserve of male staff, with games and boxing under Mr Keegan, military and Swedish Drills under Mr Cowan, football under Mr Clouston and rifle shooting under Chief Petty Officer Pickard, while Sergeant Holden was sports coach and Mr Rowley taught carpentry. In the wake of the Boer War a number of prep schools adopted rifle shooting, though the Arnold House prospectus reassured parents that safety was a paramount consideration. The School used the miniature rifle range belonging to the Central Electric Light Company, with weekly instruction being given in military and sporting rifles. The prospectus noted that the School 'has use of an American sub-target machine (with which no shots are fired). Boys use this until they are skilled in aiming and have mastered the etiquette of fixing point.' Scout troops were also popular following the foundation of the scouting movement by Baden-Powell after the Boer War, and a troop was formed at Arnold House in 1909. It was short-lived but reappeared as the 9th Marylebone Troop in 1918.

ARNOLD HOUSE SCHOOL,
1, LOUDOUN ROAD, N.W.

Programme of

DRILLING DEMONSTRATION.

JUNIORS:
Marching.
Exercises.
Game—" Statues." (*Object: Control, balance and appreciation of form.*)
Galloping Ponies.

MIDDLE SCHOOL:
Elementary Military Marching and Squad Formations.
Swedish Gymnastic Lesson. (*See pamphlet.*)
Game—" Ninepins." (*Object: Lightness and quickness.*)

SENIORS:
Military Marching and Squad Formations.
Clearing an Obstacle.
Swedish Gymnastic Lesson. (*See pamphlet.*)
Game—" Hit the Duffer." (*Object: Alertness.*)

WHOLE SCHOOL:
Group.

God Save the King

** *These School Demonstrations are of educational rather than of spectacular interest. They are to show the work of the whole class, and not the work of picked boys.*

JULY 22ND, 1916.

Cricket and football were played every afternoon, using the grounds in Regent's Park, while senior boys travelled to a playing field leased by the School at Wembley Park. The boys wore grey flannels, a red blazer and brown rubber shoes for cricket, and for football and gymnastics a green jersey and blue serge knickerbockers. Red and green were the School colours, with the former later influencing Miss Hanson's choice of School flower, the scarlet carnation, in 1920. The first School football match appears to have been a goalless draw against Frethern House in 1907, and the first cricket matches took place the following summer, with Arnold House losing away matches against Loudoun House and Upton House but winning the return fixtures at home.

ARNOLD HOUSE SCHOOL

. . MAGAZINE . .

SEPTEMBER, 1912.   No. 1.

NOTES AND NEWS.

The Summer Term of 1912 will long be remembered for its good cricket and its good work. The XI lost one match only ; and five Public School Scholarships were gained.

The Second House has moved its quarters from 22 to 17, St. Ann's Terrace. The house looks so beautifully fresh, and the garden is so pretty, that we are sorry the majority of the visitors never see " the other house."

No more suitable School House has yet turned up, for landlords object to us as tenants, nor can we find any house with such a delightful playground ; so until *the* house turns up in our immediate neighbourhood, we must be content to live under two roofs.

The whooping cough scare during the summer turned out to be *only* a scare, no second case occuring.

The School now possesses a large and very beautiful photograph of Dr. Arnold of Rugby, and for this we are indebted to Miss F. Arnold-Forster, who has sent us a copy of the picture that is in the drawing room at Fox How.

Miss Arnold has sent us a copy of Dr. Arnold's Lectures on Modern History, published now for the first time.

Prize Giving

Prize Giving was the main arena for displaying the boys' skills in public. For many years it was held in the nearby Wellington Hall in Grove End Road where 300 people crammed into the building in 1912. A programme for 1908, when the event was held in December for the first time, as it was for more than 80 years, lists two short French dramas, recitations, an Irish jig, and displays of boxing, dumb bells, club swinging and Swedish Drill. There was a whole host of prizes for school work, holiday work and conduct. A system of tickets rewarded boys for class work and conduct, with prizes for those holding the most tickets. Other than at Prize Giving there were no plays or concerts, with the first organised School concerts taking place as fund-raising events during the First World War. In 1906 there had been a hobbies exhibition, a popular activity in many boys' schools, with prizes for best collection and best original work, but it was never repeated.

Amy Hanson and the School, 1916

4.45—6.45 p.m.
Dec. 16th, 1908.

ARNOLD HOUSE SCHOOL.

51, WELLINGTON ROAD, N.W.

Swedish Drill ... Miss HASELDEN-BRETELL.
Clubs and Dumb-bells ... L. H. KEEGAN, Esq.

Boxing Contests.

Referee ... J. WARREN CLOUSTON, Esq., B.Sc.
Judges ... JOHN CHAMPNEYS, Esq. & E. CLOUSTON, Esq.

Christmas Term.

ARNOLD HOUSE SCHOOL.

. PRIZE CERTIFICATE .

Awarded in lieu of a Prize,

CHRISTMAS, 1914

(When, during The Great War the boys of the School gave up their prizes in order to help the Funds of King George Hospital for the Wounded).

To

S Naylor Smith

For

Upper III Remove Form & Examination

A. M. Hanson *Head.*

1, LOUDOUN ROAD,
ST. JOHN'S WOOD, LONDON.

Recitations.

White ...	"The Battle of Alma"	*Lushington*
Green ...	"To-day and To-morrow"	*Mackay*
Benjamin ...	"The Passing of Arthur"	*Tennyson*
Turney ...	"The Camel's Hump"	*Rudyard Kipling*
Stephenson i ...	"The Welsh Rabbit"	*Anon*
Segundo ii ...	"Drake's Drum"	*Henry Newbolt*
Stephenson ii & Burns ii ...	"Jái du bon tabac"	
Parkinson ...	"Play the game"	*Henry Newbolt*

French Play.

Les Petits Chasseurs des Rues.

Henriette (une bonne)	...	Hussey.
Alice (une méchante petite fille)	...	Eady.
Pierre (un méchant petit garcon)	...	Cock.
Jean (Petit marchand de sucre d'orge)		Segundo i.
Louisa (Petite marchande de violette)		Morgan.
Charles (un pauvre)	...	Andrade.
Jacques (un balayeur)	...	Scharlieb.
Elise (une pauvre femme)	...	Burnell.

Chant ... "Au clair de la Lune" ... Fisher i & Meek.

Horatius ... Lord Macaulay.

Fisher ii, Segundo iii, Lister, Burns ii, Jebb i, Burnett, von Bohr, Ritchie & Stewart.

Parigoris ... "Les Objets trouvés" ... *Guyau*
Lister ... "Le Renard et la Cigogne" ... *La Fontaine*

Chansonnette ... Worthington, Baker ii, Lomax, Burns ii, Stephenson i, Burns ii, Burnett, Fisher ii, etc.

Jebb ii ... "If no one ever marries me"
... *L. Alma-Tadema*.

Scene from Julius Caesar. Brutus—Morgan.
Cassius—Segundo i.

French Play.

Monsieur L' Hiver.

L'Hiver	...	Bell.
Un gros garcon	...	Segundo ii
Une petite fille	...	Fisher i.
Un garcon frileux	...	Walker
Un Bébé	...	Segundo iii.
Saint Nicholas	...	Vignoles i.
Arbre de Noël	...	Burns i.
Nouvelle-Année	...	Vignoles ii.
Gâteau des rois	...	Baker i.

Interval of 10 minutes *Coffee in Lower Hall.*

DUMB BELLS	Junior School.
CLUB SWINGING	Senior School.
SWEDISH DRILL	Junior School.
SWEDISH DRILL	Senior School.

IRISH JIG.

BOXING DISPLAY AND CONTESTS.

GOD SAVE THE KING.

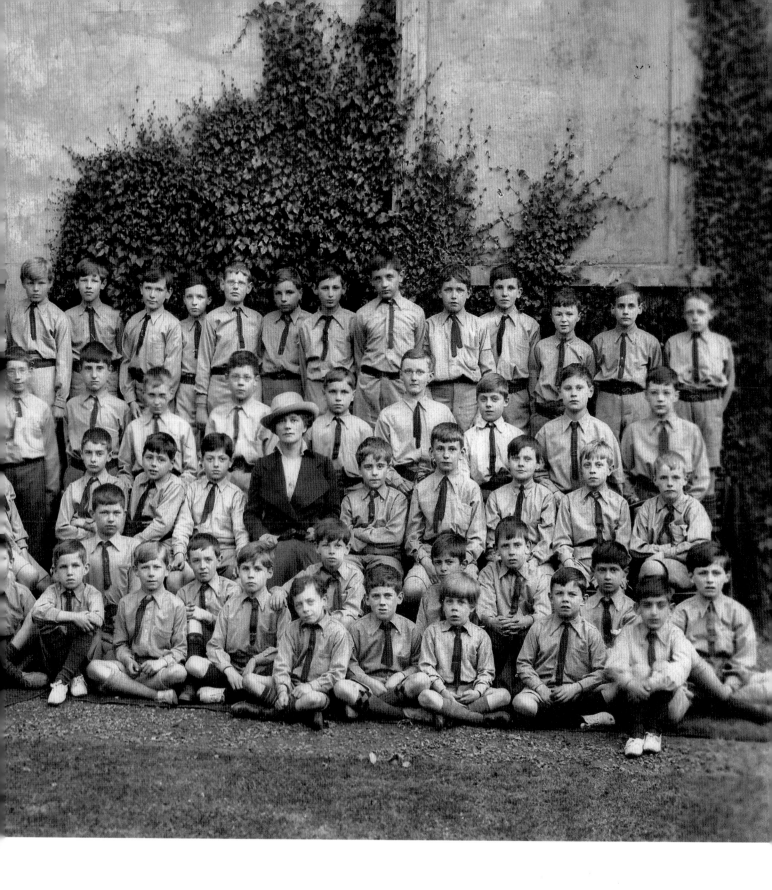

Waifs and Strays

With a view to turning the boys' charitable disposition into a habit, the School began supporting the Church of England Incorporated Society for Providing Homes for Waifs and Strays. Founded in 1881, the Society not only ran a number of homes for children in need, but also arranged places in foster homes. Arnold House supported individual boys, the first being Ernest Evans, who lived in an orphanage run by the Society in Chislehurst in Kent. In 1927 their support was transferred to another young boy, Willliam Halliwell, who lived on Tyneside. The School logbook includes a pasted-in photograph of young William, smartly dressed in sailor's smock and short trousers, holding a sailor's cap, and looking around ten or 11 years old. Three years later, the School adopted another waif, three-year-old Peter McGregor. For 14-year-old William Halliwell, unlike his peers at Arnold House, there was no opportunity for further education. School had ended and he had joined the world of work.

William Halliwell, far left, and Peter McGregor, left

Below: An advertisement for the Society

Swimming lessons were taught twice a week at the Hampstead Baths and, like a number of prep schools, Arnold House gave instruction in boxing. The prospectus stated the sport was 'one of the finest physical exercises and is also of great value in the formation of character. It teaches boys to keep their temper and to face difficulties, and, by developing physical courage, has very often proved itself the first step in the attainment of moral courage.' The School motto, chosen by Miss Hanson from a poem by Robert Herrick, also reflected this approach – 'Conquer we shall, but first we must contend, 'Tis not the strife that crowns us, but the end.' Boxing remained part of the School's out-of-class activities until the 1980s. It was coached in a local church hall, All Saints' Hall, which was also used for gym, drill, dance and carpentry, and for recreation when wet weather prevented games out of doors. Boys could also take riding lessons every Saturday morning at Hannay's Riding School, and 'small gardens are allotted to boys who have a taste for gardening'. Dancing was offered under the instruction of Miss d'Egville and her staff and class singing under Miss de Havilland Hall. If parents chose shooting, boxing, carpentry, swimming, dancing and riding for their sons, they would have paid more in extras every term than in fees.

The School motto written in the Holy Book

Hubert Green

Frederic Walker

William Chevallier Tayler

George Delmar-Williamson

Jack Tayler

Arthur William de Segundo

Above: Six of the boys who later lost their lives in or soon after the First World War, pictured at the School in 1906, below

Numbers continued to increase, reaching 75 in 1914, which included a handful of boarders, lodged in the upper floors of the house. This was a landmark year for Arnold House. Over the summer half-term weekend the School moved from Wellington Road into No. 1, Loudoun Road. Stephen Cox Newton gave up his school, selling the business and the lease on the property to Miss Hanson. Perhaps the lease on the property in Wellington Road was coming to an end, or perhaps, with rising numbers, it was becoming too small. Whatever the reason, Loudoun House now became Arnold House, and the School has remained in Loudoun Road ever since. It seems that taking over Loudoun House did not add many boys to Arnold House. It is difficult to know for sure since the prospect of further prosperity for Arnold House was dimmed in any case by the onset of war. It was later suggested that some Loudoun House parents took their sons away because the School was now run by a woman. It seems more probable that wartime uncertainty was the main reason for the fluctuation in numbers over the next few years, which reached 91 in 1917 before falling back to 51 in the following year.

Given the massive destruction London suffered from the air during the Second World War, it is easy to forget the air raids that took place during the First World War. The first raid by German airships took place on 31 May 1915, killing 28 and injuring 60. The second raid followed on 13 October when an attack by five Zeppelins, as the airships were called, killed 71 people. The event was noted in the School logbook – 'Second Zeppelin raid on London: the boarders were speedily brought downstairs from the dormitories. There was no panic at all. No damage was done in NW8, London. After the danger was over, the boys returned to bed.' Further raids brought more disruption. In June 1917, noted the logbook, 'guns and bombs dropping were heard at School', while less than a month later the entry read, 'Air raid over the City by German aeroplanes.

Returning aeroplanes seen in St John's Wood. Boarders and coaching boys were brought downstairs and collected in the corridor till the guns had stopped.' During another air raid in October the boys gathered in the kitchen just after midnight, enjoying cocoa, biscuits and chocolate provided by Matron. It was an occasion repeated several times during early 1918 and the boarders began sleeping in the School dining room. On 11 May the boarders were removed from Loudoun Road to the more distant and safer location of Northwood where a house called The Thorns was taken. A week later, noted the logbook, 'London was visited by hostile aircraft which seem to have passed over several streets near St John's Wood and done a considerable amount of damage.' Contact between the two halves of the School was kept up by regular visits from the Loudoun Road day boys who played the Northwood boarders at cricket.

The boys did their bit for the war effort. For the first Christmas of wartime, the boys despatched parcels to trawlermen on active service, wounded Belgians convalescing in a Margate hospital, men in the same company of the Artists' Rifles as Mr Mummery, who had been on the School staff, and 'to various other soldiers in whom the boys were interested'. Prize Giving was cancelled and the money saved sent to the Red Cross. Fundraising concerts included a 'Sing Song' in All Saints' Hall in December 1917, repeated a few days later in the Artists' Rifles Hospital, where each wounded soldier was given a packet of sweets.

Arnold House did its best to instil a sense of patriotism in the boys. The observance of Empire Day on 24 June, already widespread within schools before the war, was taken up by even more schools in wartime. In 1916, noted the School logbook, 'in the morning the boys all assembled in the playground to salute the flag. In the afternoon Miss Hanson gave a lecture to the whole school on the

✝

Of your Charity
Pray for the Repose of the Soul
of
Frederic Cloete Walker
(Flight Sub-Lieutenant R.N.)
Who was killed whilst flying in France,
17th March, 1917.
Aged 18 years.

✝

Eternal rest give unto him, O Lord, and let
perpetual light shine upon him.
Requiescat in Pace.

Below: Headboys Seth Dunford and Sam Sether place a wreath at the grave of Frederic Walker in the Aubigny Communal Cemetery in France, 2011

Sunday Nov. 10th 1918.

My dear Boys-

These are very solemn hours for all the world that we are passing through now - and I do not like to think that you are thoughtless and careless about them.

All the world is standing breathless as it were, waiting for the peace and the victory that perhaps God will give to us.

You must remember all the time that - if we had not been fighting in the righteous cause - and if the God of all Good had not been with us, we should have been the conquered people -. And you must remember that - we have only won this victory through years of suffering that you may never understand. - through the sacrifice and martyrdom of thousands upon thousands

Above: Extract from Miss Hanson's letter to the boys, 10 November 1918

British Empire.' In the same year a general presented the prizes at Sports Day.

The war disrupted the School's sporting activities. With the usual pitch at Primrose Hill given over to allotments, an alternative was found for junior cricket. Hockey was introduced in 1916 and the harsh winter weather in 1917 allowed Miss Hanson to take the boys skating on the lake in Regent's Park.

On 11 November 1918 the logbook recorded that 'The Armistice was signed at 5 a.m. on this day and most of the boys spent the day as spectators in the great peace rejoicings which took place in the City.' The conflict had not been without cost to Arnold House. Captain Mummery, wounded in Mesopotamia in 1916, died from flu in a German prisoner-of-war camp at the very end of the war. Throughout her life Miss Hanson kept in close touch with a number of boys after they had left Arnold House, several of whom lost their lives during the war. Arthur de Segundo, just 17, was blown up with HMS *Vanguard* in 1917. Frederic

Cloete Walker was killed at the age of 18 in 1917 when his plane crashed on take-off. In the same year Captain Hubert Green was killed in France. So too was Jack Tayler, aged 18; his brother William, having survived the war, died during the ill-fated British expedition to North Russia in 1919. George Delmar-Williamson, one of the first nine boys to join the School, survived the Western Front only to be killed in a flying accident on his return home in July 1918. Nineteen-year-old Captain John Towlson Morgan was killed just days before the war ended on 29 October 1918. This loss of life prompted Miss Hanson on the day before the Armistice to write a heart-felt address to the boys. She urged them never to forget those who had lost their lives and those they had left behind. 'You can never repay your debts,' she wrote, 'none of us can – so from this time forth – right – and your country – and your homes must be the dearest things to you on earth – for they were bought for you with such a terrible price.' Some years later, on 26 October 1926, the lost lives of Miss Hanson's precious boys were commemorated through the dedication of a war memorial in St Cyprian's in Clarence Gate, the church where Miss Hanson was a long-standing member of the congregation.

Right: The memorial plaque in St Cyprian's

PRAY FOR THE BOYS OF ARNOLD HOUSE SCHOOL who also gave their lives in the war.
H. GREEN J. T. MORGAN
A. W. DE SEGUNDO
J. A. & W. U. CHEVALLIER TAYLER
F. C. WALKER & L. HANSFORD WHITE
C. F. DELMAR-WILLIAMSON
To whose memory the screen panel of Saint Michael is dedicated.

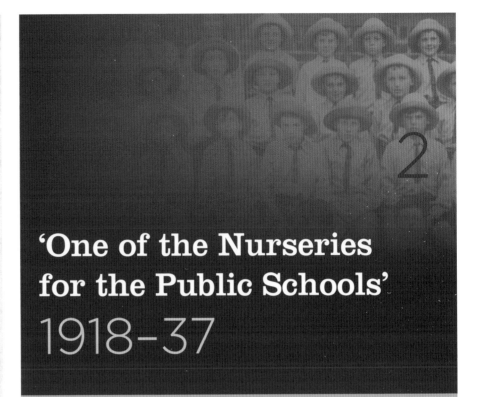

'One of the Nurseries for the Public Schools'
1918-37

During the 20 years from the end of the war the number of boys at Arnold House trebled. In 1918 there were just 51 boys at the School but this number had doubled by 1920. From 1919 to 1929 there were on average 106 boys although numbers fluctuated between 92 and 123. With such volatility it cannot have been easy running the School in what were difficult economic times. Although the immediate post-war boom encouraged a spate of new prep schools, the bust that followed brought for many others a lingering decline that often ended either in closure or amalgamation. Miss Hanson's great achievement during the last years of her tenure was to secure the future of Arnold House.

The first challenge faced by the School was the great Spanish flu epidemic of 1918-9 that killed 40 million people worldwide and an estimated quarter of a million in the UK. It was a devastating virus. A person waking up healthy in the morning could be struck dead by the evening. At Arnold House it made its first appearance among the

Arnold House School from The Cottage, late 1920s

boarders at Northwood in the summer of 1918. Absences at Loudoun Road escalated during the winter of 1919 as more and more day boys succumbed, although there were no fatalities. Unlike many other schools up and down the country Arnold House never closed.

The school inspection Miss Hanson had first sought before the war took place in May 1921. It gave Arnold House a glowing report. The inspectors concluded that 'the School is honestly fulfilling its purpose and doing good work in preparing boys for the Public Schools. The tone of the School is excellent. The health and general welfare of the pupils are regarded as of the first importance, and no pains are spared in bringing the School up to date.' Much of this, they observed, was attributable to Miss Hanson. She was 'an effective teacher and has a complete grip of work in all departments. The

excellent tone and air of refinement present in the School are due in large measure to her influence.' While the qualifications and experience of the six regular and nine occasional staff were limited, 'they are keen and promising'. This was reflected in the variable quality of the teaching. French, for instance, was excellent, while science, which was only 'taught occasionally on wet half-holidays', reflected the desperate state of the subject in most prep schools. Of the 100 boys, 20 were boarders, while the rest were drawn from London, a third from St Marylebone. Eighty per cent of them came from professional parental backgrounds.

Miss Hanson dominated the School. It was hers, after all. In the few surviving photographs of her she is wrapped up in furs and hidden in the hats popular at the time. One boy remembered that her favourite colours appeared to be mauve or lilac

Old boy correspondence

Pasted into the School logbooks are innumerable cards and letters Miss Hanson received over the years from former pupils. There are also menu cards for the 21st-birthday celebrations of boys up at Oxford and Cambridge and orders of service from weddings she had attended. It was a loyalty that several of her successors cultivated (although they never quite achieved the same intensity).

Invitation, letter, photographs and Christmas cards from former pupils

and several broad gold rings adorned her pale, slightly plump hands. Successive inspectors praised her leadership and her teaching. A confidential remark by the lead inspector for the 1930 inspection revealed something about her character. 'The HM is fussy and very talkative ... she is always busying herself about something, I am sure. And she is in many ways a good school mistress.' A deeply religious, moral and patriotic woman, she never lost her close interest in the success and future of boys who passed through the School. When she was absent from school she missed the boys. After a bout of ill health in 1925–6, she insisted on presenting the prizes at a rescheduled ceremony held in February rather than December as was traditional since, the logbook recorded, 'she had

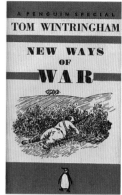

Tom Wintringham, and his 1940 book, *New Ways of War*

not been much with the boys'. As was common in many schools, the head's birthday, in Miss Hanson's case on 14 June, was a cause for a celebration among the boys. Rowland Whitehead, who with his twin brother joined the School in 1937, recalled an invitation to attend afternoon tea with Miss Hanson, 'with fine china and silver pot with silver strainer; she had a plate of long and thin-leafed lettuce upon which she sprinkled sugar!' The evening following Prize Giving in 1931 the dozen or so former pupils who attended returned to the School for supper with Miss Hanson and the staff, following which, recorded the log book, 'everyone went up to the dormitories with the band instruments and serenaded Matron and the boarders with carols. The result was a hearty pillow fight with honours even.'

Her strong personality did not endear her to everyone, either pupils or parents, though she remained an assiduous social networker. The contacts Miss Hanson made among the great and the good undoubtedly helped to promote and establish the School in its early years but they also imbued her with an exaggerated respect for the well-connected and titled. One boy, Dick Joyce, who was a pupil from 1933 until 1937, was unhappy at the School and disliked his Head-mistress. He recalled Miss Hanson's excitement at the admission of the son of an ambassador 'from a country whose ruler, Miss Hanson in ecstasy publicly confided, was reputed to have descended directly from the Sun God'. She was, he found, indomitable. 'She always had the last word. A year after going on to Bryanston, I wrote her a long letter to relieve the burden on my soul, or hoping to get a little doubt into hers. She replied by return of post that my letter had made her very proud, for there could be little wrong with a school that had taught its pupils to stand up to their Head like that.' Many boys had nothing other than happy memories of their time at

Arnold House. As one of them would later write, 'The most important thing about a first school is that the children on balance should enjoy it. I did and it was with no light heart that I discarded my red and green cap and packed my bags to depart for the unknown territory of a boarding preparatory school.'

Leonard Jacobs was a contemporary of Dick Joyce, and remembered how Miss Hanson 'rather hung over everything'. His mother was a remarkable woman who practised as a doctor but much to Miss Hanson's chagrin was also an active member of the Labour party, standing twice as a parliamentary candidate and becoming a member of the St Marylebone borough council. None of this improved her popularity with Miss Hanson, for whom the last straw was hearing that an Arnold House jersey had been seen for sale at the local Labour party bring-and-buy sale. A missive was soon on its way from the Headmistress, insisting that this should not happen again. One wonders what she thought about one former pupil, Tom Wintringham, a leading member of the British Communist party between the wars, who went on to help form the Common Wealth party during the Second World War and is credited with the idea which led to the creation of the United Nations Peacekeeping Forces.

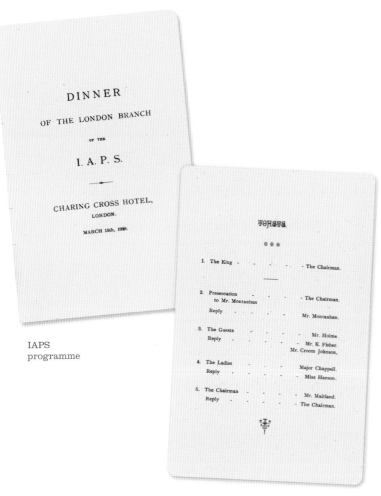

IAPS
programme

One of Miss Hanson's
'At Home' cards

A woman with less strength of personality may not have accomplished as much. Even the girls' schools that emerged during the late 19th century relied on remarkable women who needed resilience and ambition in equal measure to withstand criticism both from men and women and win the support of influential men. It was fathers not mothers in prosperous middle-class homes who by and large made the decision on where their children should attend school; this was still very much a man's world. One quirk of the School that lasted into the 1960s was the insistence that boys should address all their teachers, including women, as 'Sir'. The headmaster of Canford School, C. B. Canning, writing to Miss Hanson after presenting the prizes at Arnold House in December 1928, told her that 'a man could not have produced a school like Arnold House'. There was an element of steel in Amy Hanson's personality that was seen only occasionally. Her reputation among her male peers led her to be invited to respond to the 'Toast to the Ladies' at the London branch dinner of the IAPS in March 1928, when the principal guest was the headmaster of Oundle. She began by saying she felt 'a great honour had been done to my sex ... in allowing a woman to reply'. Highlighting the advances women had made, she subtly pointed out how able women were still patronised by men although she soothed any irritation her audience might have felt by adding, 'I do offer the grateful thanks of all women to all men for their wonderful cooperation.'

After many years as a spinster, Amy Hanson found companionship in marriage during the 1920s. Her husband, William Montagu Hunt, a widower who was a district auditor for the Ministry of Health, was a distant figure seen only occasionally at the School. He retained a flat in Hampstead and during the week in term-time she continued to live in the School. They remained together until Hunt's death in 1945. She survived her husband by two years.

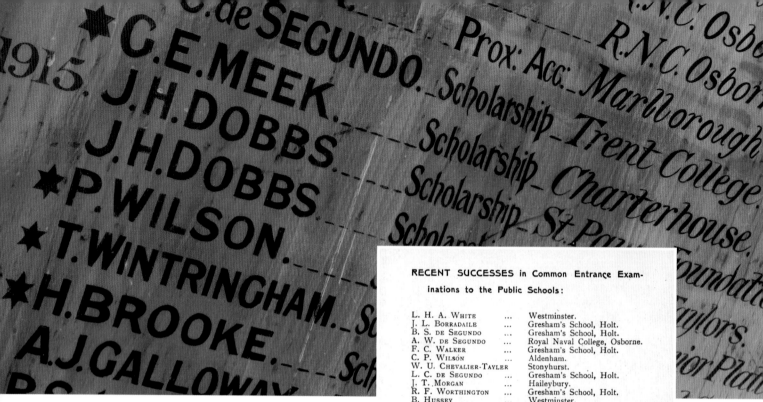

The School thrived because it produced boys to whom heads of leading public schools were happy to award places and scholarships. In 1919 Lord Clwyd told the audience at Prize Giving that the School was 'one of the nurseries for the Public Schools'. Miss Hanson told parents at Prize Giving in 1922 that public-school headmasters liked Arnold House boys because they were reliable, worked hard, came with character and personality and exerted a good influence over their peers. She put great effort into persuading parents to consider which senior schools best suited their sons. 'Boys who have no special bent for actual lessons', she told them on the same occasion, 'who are by no means fools and are clever in other ways ought to be sent to smaller schools where more individual attention is given and there is more scope for them.'

Arnold House boys went to the best schools. Shortly before the end of the war, the boarders in Northwood celebrated the success of five of their peers in winning places at Eton, Winchester, Marlborough, Radley and Gresham's. In 1920 the list also included Aldenham, Beaumont, Cheltenham, Epsom, Felsted, Harrow, Lancing, The Leys, Stonyhurst, St Paul's, Tonbridge, University College School (UCS), Wellington College and Westminster.

The School has prepared boys for entry to major public schools throughout its history

Richard Spilsbury
(top) and David
Lloyd-George, 1931

In 1923 one boy, Martens, left to become one of the first pupils at the new public school at Stowe whose foundation had been actively supported by prep schools which at the time had more boys than there were places in public schools. Arnold House had a creditable record in achieving scholarships, securing 21 between 1927 and 1936 as well as one Royal Naval Cadetship. The school inspectors, returning to Arnold House in 1930, reported that 'The standard aimed at may be stated briefly by saying that a boy in the highest Form but one would be expected to pass the Common Entrance Examination, and that a boy in the top Form should be certain of doing so. There is no Scholarship Form pure and simple, but Scholarship work is done, and a good many Scholarships have been won.'

Miss Hanson persuaded a long list of serving heads to act as referees for the School, including those from Bryanston, Rugby, Sedbergh, Stowe and Westminster. She continued to enlist the support of distinguished parents and former parents. Among them were innumerable knights and a sprinkling of peers, including several distinguished lawyers and physicians as well as the famous pathologist Sir Bernard Spilsbury, whose youngest son was head boy and won a scholarship to Sedbergh. They included the politicians Clement Davies, who later became leader of the Liberal party, and Gwilym Lloyd-George, the younger son of the former leader of the Liberal party. Miss Hanson never hesitated to invite such individuals to present the prizes. Sir James Galloway, who presented the prizes in 1921, told her that the combination of a female head with female staff teaching young boys had proved ideal for his own two sons. During the 1930s she welcomed the publicity from having a string of well-connected pupils. Among them was the young Sir Robert Peel, the sixth and last baronet, a direct descendant of the famous prime minister. His mother was the actress Beatrice Lillie and her son succeeded to the

Classrooms,
late 1920s

Jiro Matsudaira, son of the Japanese ambassador, 1935

Thank you so much for the Sports programe you sent me. So sorry I could not thank you at once but I was in hospital cutting my tonsils.

baronetcy on the death of his father in the arms of his mistress, something Miss Hanson would have preferred not to know. There was the son of the Japanese ambassador as well as the son of a well-known Greek shipping family, Lykiardopulo, whose attendance at the wedding of Prince George and Princess Marina of Greece in 1934 won a day's holiday for the rest of the School. From the copious cuttings glued into the logbook she even relished the reflected glory given to Arnold House by the incredibly popular child actor, Hughie Green, even though Green was less than enthusiastic about the School. Writing his own column in the *Daily Sketch* at the age of 15 in 1935, he remarked that 'nothing particularly exciting happened there. I was, I suppose, an average schoolboy, and was known as "the boy with the best excuses"'.

The School's reputation was achieved in spite of what appear to have been quite variable standards of teaching. In 1930 the inspectors found that there had been little improvement since 1921. Miss Hanson and the senior assistant mistress, Miss

Hasencleaver, were judged the best teachers, while, 'the remainder give service which, while quite acceptable, is not, so far as the Inspectors observed, distinguished'. While only one member of staff was a graduate, this reflected the limited opportunities available to women in higher education and the inspectors acknowledged that several teachers 'are clearly better qualified than the examinations they have passed would suggest'. They were valued by Miss Hanson, who used the masculine form to describe them all when she said in 1935 that 'Only absolute devotion to boys could ever induce a man to take up the life of a Preparatory Schoolmaster with its unlimited hours and little harassing cares apart from the teaching.'

It was a time when there was still plenty of space for quirkiness in the common room. Training specifically aimed at intending prep-school teachers was limited and much of it was in the hands of the IAPS, which for so long refused to recognise prep schools led by women. Dick Joyce welcomed the geography teacher whose outline of the theories of

Hughie Green

The Whitehead twins, weekly boarders, *c.*1937

Social Credit first stirred his social conscience. Like many other boys who were at the School between the wars the teacher he remembered above all others was Miss Marguerite Hasencleaver. A small, sparrow-like woman, whose wrinkles later earned her the nickname 'Crab Apple', she joined the staff in 1918 when she was already in her early 30s and retired in 1957 when she was 72 years old. A strict disciplinarian with a dry sense of humour, she was a brilliant mathematician. She had studied part-time over several years at the Regent Street Poly-technic although she never gained a degree. For many boys the realisation that there was joy in mathematics came in Miss Hasencleaver's classes. Another singular aspect of the teaching between the wars was the employment of a succession of native French speakers to teach the language. One of them, Mademoiselle Duhaldeborde, had a letter printed in the *Daily Telegraph* on 12 December 1931 contesting the widely held view that the English found learning a foreign language difficult. At Arnold House, she wrote, she had been 'impressed with the grounding given to small boys by the teachers in English and Latin, thus making the teaching of French to them comparatively easy work. These boys leave the School able to converse fluently on everyday subjects.' The School exhibited

some less enlightened tendencies. One old boy, C. O'Neil, who wrote that he had been forced unsuccessfully by his nurse at home to write with his right hand when he was naturally left-handed, continued that 'a few years later I went through the same futile torture at my private school'. A former pupil who contributed anonymously to the School magazine many years later recalled that there was far too much learning by rote but that at least there was an emphasis on the carrot rather than the stick, with a profusion of prizes to encourage boys in their studies.

Miss Hanson had managed to build up num-bers to 140 by 1929 but the onset of the Great Depression made this figure impossible to sustain. Numbers dipped and would not exceed 140 until 1934. This probably accounts for the fact that in 1937 fees in real terms were less than they had been when the School opened. The financial management of the School cannot have been an easy task. A shortage of money was obvious even to some of the boys. Rowland Whitehead, who entered the School in 1937, remembered that 'the School was distinctly shabby in an agreeable sort of way. The wooden floors were constantly scrubbed with red carbolic soap whose smell lingered in the air, the classrooms were dusty in the corners, the garden to the small "Shell" house, backing on to Circus Road, was unkempt and the path was cinders or very cracked crazy paving. If roses were planted in the flower beds they surely stood no chance.'

Boarding in particular was in decline. Numbers had never been great, no more than 20 boys out of 100 after the war, but in 1930 they represented less than ten per cent of the 137 boys. In 1919 the half-dozen boarders still at the School for the Peace Celebrations in the capital on 19 July were taken to watch the procession and allowed to stay up to see the fireworks in the evening. In the following year the boarders finally returned from Northwood. A regular event for the boarders was Bonfire Night,

Scout group, 1920s

when the bonfire was accompanied by fireworks and Matron supplied food, with the evening ending with a singsong around the fire. Miss Hanson and her staff tried hard to organise activities for those boys who spent their weekends and often their half-terms at School. The boarders seem to have enjoyed a wide variety of excursions. In 1921, for instance, they were given a day out over the Easter weekend, recorded in the School logbook: 'After an attempt to catch a train from Marylebone which was not running the boys with many baskets of sandwiches, set off from Marlborough Road to Northwood. After buying quantities of fruit and sweets, a visit to Mr and Mrs Tolman at the Laurels was suggested. ... Then the Gravel Pits required attention. Scouting and voyages of discovery were quickly to the fore. Lunch – a wonderful meal – followed. Games and fencing with primative [sic] weapons completed the afternoon, and on returning to School Bagattell [sic] (an old favourite) brought a very pleasant day to an end.' A boy's birthday was not allowed to pass without celebration. For the birthday of a boy named Musson in February 1923, 'a long table in the centre of the [dining] room [was] laden with as many good things as a healthy schoolboy could

Uniform

As the Depression worsened, Miss Hanson understood that some parents were in straitened circumstances. When a number of boys began taking too many liberties with the grey flannel School uniform, she introduced a cheaper one. It was supplied by W. M. Rowe & Co. of New Bond Street, who were popular with many prep schools because of the discounts they offered. In March 1931 Miss Hanson told parents that henceforth 'there should now be no excuse for the variegated element which spoils the appearance of the School. There is a great moral asset in "Dress" which it is not wise to neglect in young boys and which goes to form many things in their characters that will stand them in good stead in later life.' A grey pullover, with a red and green border around the cuffs and the bottom, worn in winter with grey flannel shirt, shorts and blazer if needed, replaced the old-fashioned green jersey. A red and green belt, clipped with a silver snake, held up the boys'

Above: Boys in the 1920s sporting various versions of the uniform

Below: An early uniform list

DAY BOYS' OUTFIT.

SUMMER.

Grey Shirts, Grey Flannel Shorts, Red Blazer, Grey Stockings, School Tie and Belt, School Cap, Grey Sun Hat, Cricket Shoes, White Gymnasium Shoes, House Shoes.

Drab Trench or Rain Coat.

WINTER.

Grey Pullover, Grey Flannel Shorts, Grey Shirts, Drab Overcoat of the School Tweed, School Cap Football Boots, White Gymnasium Shoes, House Shoes.

In addition, a boy must keep at School a Red Sweater, a Towel taken home weekly, a Comb, and a pair of Stockings in a bag.

The Overcoats must be the uniform shades of drab.

All articles must be plainly marked with the surname.

The School Colours, Red and Green, and the Outfit, are supplied by

WM. ROWE & CO. LTD. 106 NEW BOND STREET. W.1

ARNOLD HOUSE SCHOOL.

1 LOUDOUN ROAD. SAINT JOHN'S WOOD, LONDON, N.W.8.

shorts. The lighter grey shade for flannels was retained since 'in a darker shade the boys look exactly like "the many boys in the street" who wear cheap dark readymade grey flannels'. (Miss Hanson had earlier urged, 'Will parents be good enough not to give away School uniforms to poor boys'.) Shirts were made in three thicknesses for different times of the year, one described by the High Church headmistress as 'a weight about the thickness of a nun's veil for summer'.

The School colours

The School colours made a great impression on some boys. Rowland Whitehead remembered that 'Our jerseys were red, the blankets on the beds were red, the ribbons on our grey felt sun hats were red and green as were our caps, ties and summer blazers. This is the sort of identity that young children like. I had come from schools with little formal visual identification; now this sense of colour has stayed with me – always. The green was not pea green nor blue green but an exact shade as was the red, not quite pillar box, not really carmine and no hint of orange.'

D. I. B. Maclean wearing the standardised uniform introduced in the early 1930s

ARNOLD HOUSE SCHOOL,
1 LOUDOUN ROAD,
ST. JOHN'S WOOD.

Preparatory for the Public Schools and Royal Navy.
Colours, Red & Green. Telephone, Maida Vale 3003.
For particulars apply A. M. HANSON.

wish for – jellies, fruit salads, cakes, iced buns, sandwiches etc – and last but not least was a magnificent birthday cake covered with pink icing'. The birthday tea was followed by wrestling, boxing and a skit on Romeo and Juliet, which all took place in the specially cleared fifth-form room.

Boarding remained part of School life until the Second World War. Colin Winser, who joined the School not quite aged five in 1936, recalled the top-floor dormitory in No. 1, Loudoun Road. Every now and again the boarders were required to practise their evacuation drill, descending through a canvas chute from the top window over the front door. Rowland Whitehead and his twin brother were weekly boarders and Rowland recalled that the Matron, Miss Waghorn, 'was a very large and comfortable figure who, at the end of our day, sat in an equally large and comfortable armchair with my brother and me on the floor at her feet. Thus we said our evening prayer.'

In theory the emphasis placed by Arnold House on developing the individual potential of every boy set it apart from many other prep schools of the time. In practice the extra-curricular activities offered by Arnold House differed little from other schools. Team sport tended to dominate out of class activities, the exception being boxing, there was little development of music and art, and other options were limited.

In 1920 the School utilised several playing fields at South Hampstead, Eastcote, Golders Green and Primrose Hill. Eastcote was the usual venue for the annual Sports Day. Matches were played against St Paul's Cathedral Choir School, All Saints' Choir School, Tenterden House, Frethern House, Northwood Prep School, The Hall and St John's, Pinner, amongst others. A series of report books, describing every School match, began in 1920 with a report on the cricket match against St Paul's Cathedral Choir School on 3 June – 'Played at Bellingham, this match resulted in a draw. The

Above: A School concert in the playground, 1934

Left: Pupils waiting for the Swedish Drill cup to be awarded by Miss Hanson, 1932

Choir School won the toss and collected 149 runs for 5 wickets before declaring. By careful and correct cricket, Arnold House replied with 59 for 5 wickets (Clover Brown 17).' The game was treated with the utmost seriousness. In 1923 a schedule of fines and incentives was in operation, with deductions for bad shots or poor calling or running away from the ball and rewards for excellent batting and outstanding fielding. In the days when the city could be blanketed in a thick stifling carpet of smog that blotted out the light, it was not uncommon for a typical entry in the logbook to read, as it did in November 1926, 'Thick fog – match against St John's cancelled'.

Hockey, initiated during the war, was revived in 1926, as was rugby in 1929, but matches were never played against other schools.

Boxing

Boxing at Arnold House was probably at the peak of its popularity between the wars. Half the School was taking part in 1920, when the long-serving coach, George Penny, gave instruction twice a week. Penny was a noted champion boxer who had won the lightweight championship Coronation Belt in 1902 and was sought after by many boxing clubs. He was succeeded by Dave Barry, whose death in 1934 led to the long involvement of the Gutteridge family with the School.

Boxing was held in the semi-basement of the building on the edge of the Loudoun Road site in Grove End Road known as The Cottage, which acted for many years as the junior school. (The St John's Wood Synagogue now stands on the site.) The winner of the annual competition, held for some years at the Belsize Boxing Club in Finchley Road, was awarded what was known as 'the golden glove'. It was a testing sport for many boys. One former pupil later recorded how as a small boy he had returned home in tears, 'having received a stern reprimand from our burly instructor for hitting him below the belt. Very reasonably, I pleaded that at my height it was impossible to reach above the lofty belt.'

Above: Boxing team, *c.* late 1920s/early 1930s

Right: Programme for the School boxing competitions, 1930

Above: Arthur Gutteridge with his sons, Dick and Jack ('the Gutteridge Twins')

Right: An advertising card for Jack Gutteridge

PHONE: CLERKENWELL 4605.

JACK GUTTERIDGE,

PREMIER

Boxing Trainer, Second and Masseur

to N.S.C. and B.B.B.C.

33. BRITANNI▢ ▢W,
ESSEX ROAD ▢ ▢N. N.1

Late Boxer,

Winner of 4 Army 9st. Championships
and over 100 Fights.

Trainer and Sparring Partner to
PRIMO CARNERA, 1932.

Instructor St. Brides B.C. 14 years.

Instructor Arnold House School,

Instructor Men's Institute, 10 years.

Late 9st. Champion East Coast, 1916.

Lightweight Champion
Northern Command, 1917.

Winner 57th Divisional Championships.

Champion Northern France, 1918.

Trainer to noted Champions.

Licensed Agent BBBC.   Broadcast 1935

To Parents and all friends.   **Please bring this.**

ARNOLD HOUSE SCHOOL

BOXING COMPETITIONS

for

THE MARSHALL CUP (Lightweight).

Cemyln-Jones *v.* Corcos ii.   Reynell ii. *v.* Wintringham
Allen i. *v.* Parker ii.   Allen ii. *v.* Ward iii.

THE HEAD CUP (Featherweight).

West-Russell *v.* Leveaux i.   Lane *v.* Ackner ii.
Batty-Shaw *v.* Allen iii.

THE PRITCHARD CUP (Middleweight).

Bucklow *v.* Dunkels   Dix *v.* Abel i.
Gilliam ii., a bye.

THE GRAVES CUP (Heavyweight)

Sheldon *v.* Benjamin   Reynell i. *v.* Ackner i.
Watt ii. *v.* Walker iii.

THE NEVILLE CUP—Inter House.

to be held at

The Drill Hall, Henry Street, St. John's Wood

(By kind permission of the Officer commanding 23rd
Armoured Cars)

on

WEDNESDAY, 3rd DECEMBER, 1930,

(3 to 5 o'clock)

Referee :

PROFESSOR GEORGE PENNY

Late Instructor to 1st Batt. Irish Guards, Belsize Boxing
Club, London Hospital Students (20 years), Arnold House
School (20 years), Winner of 57 contests and the Light-
weight Championship Coronation Belt at the New
Adelphi Club (1902).

Judges :

Sergt. J. J. STEDMAN, "J" Battery R.H.A.
Runner-up Heavyweight Championship, Egypt.

F. NEWSOME, Esq.

Seconds :

PROFESSOR A. WHEELER

Instructor to Arnold House School
Winner of Army and Navy 9-stone Championship at
Aldershot (1900), and of over 50 contests. For many years
Instructor to the King's Royal Rifles and other Clubs.

PROFESSOR PENNY.

Timekeeper :

Lieut.-Comdr. R. MAITLAND MAKGILL CRICHTON, R.N.

M.C. : CAPTAIN COLIN CAMPBELL.

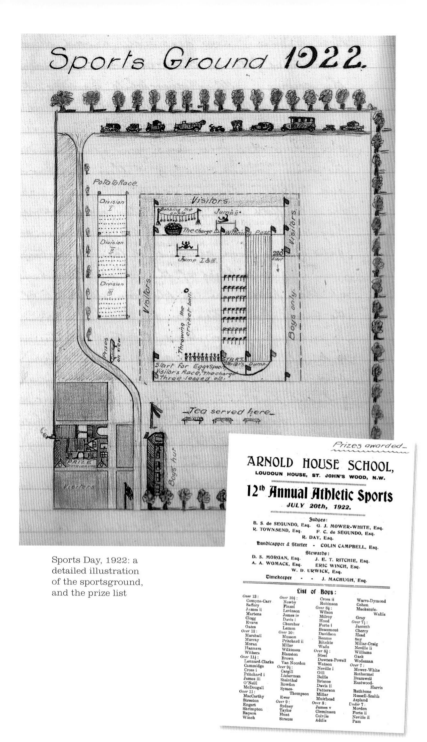

Sports Ground 1922.

Potato Race.

Division I
Division II
Division III

Prizes on view

Visitors

Bobbing the apple
Jump II.
The charge
Winning Post
Jump I & II.
Throwing the cricket ball
Barriers
Dump
Start for Egg&Spoon, Visitors Race, The charge, Three-legged etc.

220 yds

Visitors

Boys only.

Tea served here.

PRIZE
Visitors
Boys hut

ARNOLD HOUSE SCHOOL,
LOUDOUN HOUSE, ST. JOHN'S WOOD, N.W.

Prizes awarded

12th Annual Athletic Sports
JULY 20th, 1922.

Judges:
B. S. de SEGUNDO, Esq.   G. J. MOWER-WHITE, Esq.
R. TOWNSEND, Esq.   F. C. de SEGUNDO, Esq.
R. DAY, Esq.

Handicapper & Starter -   COLIN CAMPBELL, Esq.

Stewards:
D. S. MORGAN, Esq.   J. E. T. RITCHIE, Esq.
A. A. WOMACK, Esq.   ERIC WINCH, Esq.
W. D. URWICK, Esq.

Timekeeper - -   J. MACHUGH, Esq.

List of Boys:

Over 13:
Comyns-Carr
Saffery
James ii
Martens
Clegg
Evans
Oates
Over 12:
Marshall
Murray
Moran
Hannam
Withers
Over 11½:
Lennard-Clarke
Cammidge
Cross i
Pritchard i
James iii
O'Neill
McDougall
Over 11:
MacCarthy
Streeton
Engert
Shrimpton
Hapson
Winch

Over 10½:
Newby
Findal
Levinson
James iv
Davis i
Churcher
Lemon
Over 10:
Musson
Pritchard ii
Miller
Wilkinson
Blaustan
Brown
Van Noorden
Over 9½:
Cargill
Lieberman
Steinthal
Rowdon
Symes-
Thompson
Ewer
Over 9:
Sydney
Taylor
Hunt
Strauss

Cross ii
Robinson
Over 8½:
Wilson
Milroy
Hood
Forte i
Beaumont
Davidson
Beninc
Ritchie
Wade
Over 8½:
Steel
Downes-Powell
Watson
Neville i
Gill
Bellis
Briscoe
Davis ii
Patterson
Millar
Muirhead
Over 8:
James v
Clemineau
Colville
Addis

Warre-Dymond
Cohen
Mackenzie-
Wallis
Grey
Over 7½:
Jacomb
Cherry
Head
Incy
Millar-Craig
Neville ii
Williams
Gask
Wodeman
Over 7:
Mower-White
Rothermel
Bramwell
Eastwood-
Harris
Rathbone
Russell-Smith
Aspland
Under 7:
Mordon
Forte ii
Neville ii
Pam

Sports Day, 1922: a detailed illustration of the sportsground, and the prize list

One of the few deaths among boys at the School occurred after Frankie Rothschild was kicked during a game of football at the School in 1920. Following three operations, he sank into delirium and died five days later.

For internal matches the boys were divided into teams, Tigers, Lions, Wolves and Bears, a division

that would eventually lead to the creation of a house system in 1926.

Running began in 1920 with runs on Primrose Hill. There were several annual competitions in boxing, football (six-a-side), gymnastics and drill, which eventually became inter-house competitions, with the addition of hockey and swimming. Annual displays were given in drill – Miss Hanson believed that drill 'produces self-reliance, alertness, initiative and concentration of thought, in addition to a beautiful body' – and swimming. Miss Haselden-Brettell took both Swedish Drill and swimming. Leonard Jacobs recalled Miss Haselden-Brettell's curious method of teaching a boy to swim. Swimming backstroke ahead of her pupil, she kept him afloat by using her foot, with her big toe inserted in the boy's tummy button.

Apart from sport, other activities were sporadic and limited, but Arnold House was little different from many other prep schools. After the war dancing and carpentry classes were revived. The carpenter returned to the School after three years spent making aeroplanes. There were occasional lantern lectures, often organised for parents and boys, on topics like India, the Royal Navy and Napoleon. A talk about deep-sea fishermen led to the formation within the School of a branch of the Young Trawlers' Union. In 1924 one parent, the distinguished historian Arnold Toynbee, lectured on Greece and the Near East. In 1933 a talk on Stanley in Africa was illustrated with 'a talking film'. In the 1930s the local League of Nations Union held a lecture at the School. This led the School to form its own junior branch at a time when the League seemed to represent a bulwark against a future war. In 1935 a lantern lecture on Malaya gave most boys their first experience of a film in colour. The School wireless also kept the boys in touch with world events. In September 1934, for instance, they all listened to the naming and launch of the new Cunard liner, the *Queen Mary*.

Above: Cricket
dinner menus, 1923
and 1924

Below: *Pitt*
magazines, 1934
and 1935.
The cover of the
1935 edition was
drawn by J. Honour,
and the magazine
was edited by
R. W. D. Holland

Music was a neglected subject in most prep schools between the wars. At Arnold House it remained restricted mainly to singing with some instrumental performances at the annual School concert, which was generally the only forum for School drama as well. Rowland Whitehead recalled that the boys were prepared for the concert by a Dr Aitken, who insisted to Rowland and his brother that 'You two Whiteheads are not to open your mouths! You sound like foghorns and will spoil

everything!' There was a year, 1921, when the School choir entered two music festivals held in London. At the first, held in Central Hall, Westminster, the boys apparently acquitted themselves well although the logbook entry recorded that their third song 'went to pieces, chiefly J. H. Handley's fault for making them sing it without music'. Otherwise, however, the records are silent about music.

The house system, introduced in 1925, made inter-house entertainments a fixture in the School calendar, usually in the form of playlets. Each of the three houses, named after great British historical figures, had their own motto and colours. Nelson took the motto 'Facta, non Verba' and the colours blue and yellow; Wellington, 'Fidue et Audax' and light blue and dark blue; and Pitt, 'Strike Sure' and black and old gold. As well as entertainments, there were inter-house sporting competitions, and the Cock House Cup Competition was introduced, covering games, work and conduct. Pitt House was the first winner. As numbers grew, a fourth house, Thompson, with blue and white colours, was formed in 1938.

Boys were appointed as captains of each house, another layer in the hierarchy of responsibility among boys. There were also captains of each form, stretching from the junior forms via Shell to the fifth forms. The junior forms were all given names – such as St George, St Patrick, Middle, Sunshine and Cottage – which tended to change, although they would all eventually adopt saints' names, with the addition of St Andrew and St Nicholas, a practice which lasted into the 1990s. Boys could also aspire to be prefects, head prefects or head of School.

The School year was punctuated by a number of regular events. During the winter term the boys all attended the Ash Wednesday service, which for many years took place at All Saints' Church in Finchley Road. Although the School was non-denominational, it was inevitably influenced by Miss Hanson's strong High Church Anglicanism. Boys were expected to

Excursions

The School's occasional excursions engendered great excitement. There were visits to theatres and museums. The Zoo, the Tower of London and the Houses of Parliament were – and still are – regular destinations. Sometimes a handful of boys might be treated by a parent to a visit to a test match down the road at Lord's. There were evening bus rides around the bright lights of Piccadilly. In July 1922 the senior boys travelled by coach to Instone Air Station at Croydon. They visited the workshops, watched mail planes coming in to land and had tea in the waiting room where they were told it was patriotic to take an interest in flying, which was such a huge asset to the Empire. In May 1924 a visit was organised to the British Empire Exhibition. The noted architectural writer Sir Lawrence Weaver took several forms to see the famous Queen's Doll's House. He guided them through the palaces of art and industry, leaving them on their own to explore the palace of engineering.

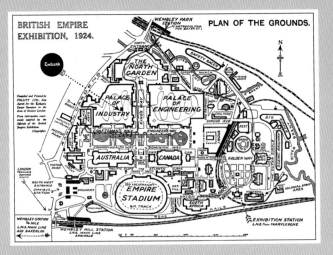

Left: Map of the British Empire Exhibition, 1924 with the boys' intended route in red

Below: Bustling crowds explore the 1924 British Empire Exhibition

attend church, even those who were Jewish or Greek Orthodox, but very few non-Anglican parents ever insisted their sons should not. For boys of successive generations, the Ash Wednesday and other services were just part of being at Arnold House. In the Summer term the two main events were the athletic sports and the observance of Empire Day. In November the boys attended an Armistice Day service. At first this was held in school, then at St Mark's Church in Hamilton Terrace, with each boy wearing a dark armband, before moving to St Cyprian's in Clarence Gate, where it remained until the 1970s and to which it returned in the 1990s. This was the church where Amy Hanson herself had worshipped since its completion in 1904. It is regarded as one of the finest examples of High Church architecture. She was closely involved with St Cyprian's, counting successive priests, particularly Father Thomas Robson, as friends. She was also a generous benefactor of the

church during her lifetime and left both the church and its incumbent considerable sums in her will.

The end of the year was marked by Common Entrance and completed by Prize Giving in December. The latter, held before the war at the Wellington Hall, was also held at the Hampstead Conservatoire before finding a home for several years from 1927 at the newly completed Rudolf Steiner Hall near Baker Street.

The tradition of charitable giving begun with the Waifs & Strays Fund during the war strengthened in peacetime, particularly as difficult economic times exposed the rising tide of poverty among the less well-off in an age before the welfare state. In 1921 boys gave toys they no longer wanted for distribution among children in London's East End. Before the war Miss Hanson had taken an interest in missionary work in Sierra Leone and successive bishops were invited to the School to talk to the

Reverend Thomas Fairfax Uphill Robson, vicar of St Cyprian's, 1935–55

boys about education there. In the 1930s the School began supporting the annual egg week organised every Easter for the Children's Hospital in Hampstead. In 1933 boys collected nearly a thousand fresh eggs.

As the British economy began to improve, numbers revived, reaching 165 in 1936. Until then accommodation at the School had been ample. In 1930 the fall in boarding numbers had allowed a former dormitory to be turned into a classroom, and a prefabricated building was erected between No. 1, Loudoun Road, and The Cottage. Space, the inspectors concluded that year, was quite satisfactory. With the addition of nearly 30 more boys over the next few years, it became somewhat less satisfactory. Miss Hanson was particularly concerned that The Cottage was no longer suitable for use as a junior school. In 1935 she began exploring the possibilities of extending the School in discussion with the Eyre Estate, the owners of the freehold of No. 1, Loudoun Road, the lease of which was soon due to expire. The Estate, then as now, proved sympathetic. The lease on No. 1 was extended by 28 years and the Estate also agreed to lease to the School from 1938 a large garden at the

rear of No. 1 to add to the existing playground. With security of tenure achieved, it was possible for Miss Hanson to acquire the new property next door at No. 3, Loudoun Road. Writing in the School magazine, the *Arnold House Chronicle*, for 1935, Miss Hanson recorded how,

> to make the purchase of No. 3 a feasible proposition I was obliged to make sure of obtaining an extended lease of No. 1, Loudoun Road. This was a very difficult process for naturally the Trustees of the Estate wanted this very valuable piece of ground for development, a much more paying investment for them. And here I must pay a tribute to the Trustees of the Eyre Estate who have undoubtedly made a sacrifice in allowing the School to continue to occupy this valuable site.

In a separate note written in February 1936, she reported on her purchase of the leasehold of No. 3, Loudoun Road. 'I hope to start there a new and very much up to date Junior School – transferring the classes from the Cottage School in 45 Grove End Road – after the Easter holidays.' On 19 May 1936 the vicar of St Cyprian's blessed the new house.

The tester in St Cyprian's in honour of Miss Hanson

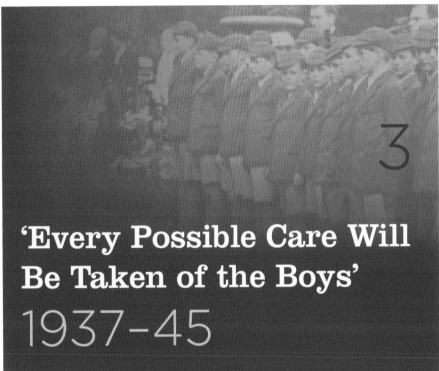

'Every Possible Care Will Be Taken of the Boys'
1937–45

Arnold House boys
on their arrival at
the Panmure Hotel,
Edzell, September
1938

In renewing the lease of No. 1, Loudoun Road, and acquiring the leasehold of No. 3, Loudoun Road, Miss Hanson was securing the future of her school. In 1936 she was 65 years old. She had dominated her staff since Miss Hughes had left in 1910. There was no one at the School either with the inclination or the funds to take over Arnold House from her. She found her successor elsewhere.

George Milne Smart, the son of a Scottish farmer, was born in Edinburgh in 1905. His mother came from the Chiene family. Her father, a partner in the Edinburgh accountancy firm of Chiene & Tait, had been one of the founders of the Edinburgh Investment Trust, established in 1889. With the independent income derived from his mother's family, George had the funds to buy Arnold House from Miss Hanson. His private funds also allowed him to underwrite the costs of running the School. And in nearly 30 years as head of Arnold House he would never draw a salary. He was, reflected one former pupil, the last of the gentlemen amateurs. For George Smart, Arnold House was almost a

George Smart.
Portrait by Diccon
Swan, 1988

hobby, but one in which he invested a great deal of time, love and devotion.

After prep school, George was educated at Fettes College in Edinburgh before reading history at Worcester College, Oxford. He entered teaching as an assistant master at Northaw prep school at Surrenden-Dering in Kent. The school had begun life in Potters Bar before moving to Kent and still flourishes, although under the name of Norman Court. There he became senior assistant master.

George Smart was the epitome of the independently wealthy British gentleman. Alan Lipscomb, who came to know him well, particularly many years later when he was chairman of governors at Arnold House, spoke of 'his standards of politeness and unfailing courtesy, his self-discipline, his attention to detail, his meticulous standard of dress. It was these qualities he sought to instil into his pupils as well as a sound foundation of learning. He was excellent company and could be very funny.' He enjoyed dining with friends at the best restaurants, where he was greeted by the head waiter and ushered to a favourite table. He loved horse-racing and late in life began owning horses, which gave him much pleasure as well as winning him money. Fluent in French, he would travel across the Channel not only to enjoy the culinary delights he found there but to visit the casinos in Deauville and Trouville.

His greatest strength as a teacher was the feeling he engendered among pupils that, as Tony Roques, who entered Arnold House in 1945, would describe it, 'you knew he was completely on your side'. He was an encouraging teacher who never hesitated to give praise. He understood boys and had a natural instinct for dealing with them. Sometimes he took older boys on one of his day trips to France, taking them out to lunch and insisting they should speak only French during the course of the meal. On leaving School, every former head boy was invited to dine with him at the Connaught. He was friendly, fair, kindly and supportive but never lax. In his presence boys at once fell silent. His appreciation of the finer things in life led him to expect high standards. Respected by the boys, he instilled in them a sense of pride and affection for the School. 'I can't think of a boy who didn't like him,' remembered Antony Japhet, who also joined the School in 1945. He was, said William Falk, who joined the School in 1949, 'a wonderful influence'. (Falk was one of four generations of the same family who came to Arnold House, stretching from Cecil in 1905 to Michael in 2008.) He believed, recalled Peter Rawlins, a boy at the School in the late 1950s, in a traditional liberal education, encouraged hard work and hated indolence. Arnold House, said Rawlins, 'was a very happy place made in his image and to his high standards'. Like Miss Hanson, he took a deep interest in boys after they left Arnold House. He had the knack of recognising boys even decades after they had left and recalling at once everything about them.

He was a man who possessed charm in abundance which never failed to cast its spell over parents, especially mothers. For Tony Roques, 'his greatest gift with parents was in making them think he

Above: An invitation to the 'At Home' at which Miss Hanson introduced George Smart to parents

Right: Note to parents about Mr Smart after his first year at the school

ABOUT MR. SMART

This is the end of the first year that Mr. Smart has been with us. I should like to say that we all very much enjoy having him with us. It was with great misgivings and with faint hope that I began the search for someone to share my work and responsibilities. However, Mr. Smart has come into the School with such an open mind, and a happy spirit of cheerful co-operation that the misgivings were soon dissipated. And as the year has gone on I have felt how fortunate the School is in having a second Head, a man who has every gift of youth, character and intellect, and who will help us to maintain in its fullest - all the traditions and the greatness of the School.

The thing that has been nearest my heart in making the decision to take a partner, has been the welfare of the boys, and, if I may call it so, "the Soul of the School. But I have faith that the little stream of Arnold House Boys will long go forth into the world - purposeful, having the right values and full of human kindliness.

He will not have the thrill of making the School from the beginning - waiting with no boys at all ¢ begging the first and buying the second for a golden half-sovereign, but I hope as time goes on, he will feel as I so often feel, that the "Lot has fallen to me in a fair ground, in a fair ground," in the School in St. John's Wood.

thought their boy was the only one who really mattered'. Perhaps it was this charm, on top of every other advantage he seemed to have, that persuaded Amy Hanson that George Smart was the right person to take over Arnold House.

For Smart, Arnold House, after many years under Miss Hanson, was ripe for him to make his mark upon it. He would also have appreciated its location in leafy and prosperous St John's Wood, close to the delights of the capital, and its reputation as a fashionable school for the wealthy, affluent and socially well-connected. This, after all, was the school of choice for the Pitamber Shum Shere, the son of Prince and Princess Bishnu of Nepal.

George Smart was introduced to parents in the late spring of 1937. An invitation dated 26 May read 'Mr and Mrs Montagu Hunt [and] Mr George Smart at Home at Three Loudoun Road'. For two years Amy Hanson and George Smart worked alongside each other. Miss Hanson intended to hand over completely in 1939, and George Smart did indeed become de facto Headmaster, but Miss Hanson's involvement with Arnold House continued during the first few difficult years of the war.

For boys at the time, George Smart represented a clear break with the past. Roger Langrish, who later taught at the School, remembered how Smart 'was to us boys a ray of light, for he had a puckish sense of humour; his lessons were both businesslike and full of fun, in sharp contrast to the austere Hanson approach'.

with their work'. The following day a supplementary notice was issued. The Loudoun Road school would remain open for the boys of families who wished them to remain in London but boys travelling to Scotland were asked to be on the platform at Euston station by seven o'clock that evening. No sooner had the School party reached their destination after a slow and wearisome journey of many hours than the crisis had passed. As Smart later wrote, 'it had been quite exhausting enough making all the plans for evacuation and executing them, without having to face an immediate return, so the boys and staff enjoyed what was more or less a fortnight's holiday in Scotland in term time'. Leonard Jacobs was among the evacuees and his

Left: Frederick Selby

Below: Letter informing parents of plans to evacuate to Scotland, September 1938

There was little time for George Smart to settle in. This was a period dominated by the approaching storm of another European conflict. The School welcomed a few refugees from Nazi Germany. One boy who left Germany as Fritz Peter Seelberg became first Fred Selberg and finally Frederick Selby. 'Arnold House,' he recalled, 'accepted me, though I spoke little English.' The first real scare came with the Munich crisis in the late summer of 1938. War appeared imminent and was averted only by the agreement signed between the United Kingdom and Germany on 30 September. Smart and Miss Hanson were in complete agreement that in the event of war the School should be evacuated to a safer area. A notice issued on 26 September announced that the School would close at once in the event of general mobilisation and would take over the Panmure Arms hotel in Edzell, 50 miles north of Perth. The hotel, which still flourishes today, was close to George Smart's own house. It was a location, stressed the notice, where safety, food and quiet were all assured – 'the boys need know little of the war and should be able to get on

ARNOLD HOUSE SCHOOL
SAINT JOHN'S WOOD
N.W.8.

26th September 1938

In the event of general mobilisation the School here will be immediately closed. We have made arrangements to take over an hotel in Scotland about 50 miles beyond Perth. It is considered one of the safest places in the British Isles, and we are assured on good authority that there will be greater food facilities there than in England, and certainly it will be a restful and quiet spot – the boys need know little of the war and should be able to get on with their work. The place has the added advantage of being near to Mr. Smart's home and he and his people are well known in the village.

We are making a special inclusive fee of 45 guineas per term. Payments already made this term will be treated as on account.

Will those parents who wish to send their boys please let us know at once so that other necessary arrangements can be made. This is urgent.

Evacuation to Edzell, 1938.

Below: Arnold House boys during the journey north:
1. Wakely
2. Unknown
3. Reid II
4. Lloyd-George
5. Foxley
6. Davies
7. Morris III
8. Morris I
9. Reid I
10. Sarson
11. Dickinson I
12. Golodetz

A Tribute to Edzell

Poem by Maurice Temple Smith (age 12)
Arnold House

There stands among the peaceful Scottish hills,
Set in the meadows green and cornfields gold,
Amongst the glens and sparkling little rills,
A village picturesque and old.

Past it a river flows along its course,
Sometimes a cauldron boiling white with foam,
Next moment quiet – next with sombre force
It rushes onward past its Scottish home.

A village still unmoved by troublous times,
A peaceful refuge in a world of hate,
As Edzell Church sends forth its silver chimes
It seems that little villages are great.

The Panmure Arms
Hotel, Edzell

only memory is 'the shock of going from a day school to a boarding school'. Before he left in the following year, he featured as Prime Minister Neville Chamberlain in a short play based on Munich presented at his last School concert. Rowland Whitehead recalled that the hotel was 'rather grand, set at the end of the village whence an open road led to who knows where. Pine trees gave off a delicious scent. The air was crisp and clean. The Finchley Road seemed aeons away. Lessons were conducted in the dining room after breakfast and the smell of hot rolls lingered. The napkins and tablecloths were starched.' At first, Colin Winser remembered, boys were reluctantly forced to share beds. Contrary to the hopes expressed by the School, little work was done at the hotel, which was too small and had limited facilities.

On 6 October 1938 parents received another notice. 'The International Situation having cleared and facilities for travel again being normal it is considered wise to return to London at the beginning of next week.' Buses would take boys from the hotel to the station at Brechin. The railway company had made special arrangements to put on sleeping cars which would later be attached to the night train at the Bridge of Dun on 11 October. The boys were met by their parents at Euston the following day.

The respite from war was brief. On 25 July 1939 a small group of boys participated in one of the last peacetime School events. They had been invited to form part of the guard of honour for the Queen at the garden party she attended at Grove House, Regent's Park. Funds were being raised for the St Marylebone Housing Association Building Fund, of which Miss Hanson was a patron and to which she, George Smart and the boys had contributed £20.

Less than a month later evacuation plans were dusted off once more. On 24 August 1939 parents were told that George Smart was already waiting at the Panmure Arms to receive any boys whose parents wished to send them to Edzell in advance of the start of term. War was declared on 3 September. On 19 September an escort was provided to take boys up to Scotland by the evening express from Euston. It also called at Bletchley, regarded as a safer location outside London, where more boys were met by Miss Hanson and other members of staff. All the boys were asked to take with them blankets, sheets and

Arnold House boys form a guard of honour at the Queen's Garden Party, Grove House, Regent's Park, 1939

towels. Sixty of them, just a third of the School roll, made the journey. Many others remained on holiday with their parents.

Tony Foxley was one of the boys in the party that arrived in Edzell. He recalled, 'Some of us were taken for a treat to Mrs Smart Senior's home in Easter Ogil, not so far away, where she had this tree with very soft bark that we could punch without damaging our fists. Mrs Smart also ran a knitting

ARNOLD HOUSE SCHOOL,
SAINT JOHN'S WOOD, N.W.8.

As a state of War now unhappily exists the School as previously announced will re-open on September 20th at the Panmure Hotel, Edzell, Angus, Scotland.

An escort will be provided to take the boys to Edzell on Tuesday, September 19th. We think it is advisable for the boys to meet and travel North together from a place outside the London area -- Bletchley is under consideration as the most convenient station. The boys could there join the Scottish Express at 8.41 p.m. (Euston 7.40) and travel through to Scotland. (The train could also be joined at Rugby.)

The Railway Authorities hope to provide sleepers again as they did last September, but they must know the numbers at once if this is to be arranged by the 19th. Will you kindly reply on the enclosed postcard, if possible by return of post.

Miss Hanson hopes to be at Bletchley by 5 o'clock on September 19th with members of the staff to meet the boys and take them to Scotland. Mr. Smart will meet them at Bridge O'Dun. Precise details will be sent later. The urgent thing now is for the Railway Company to know the numbers.

Mr. Masters is still at 1, Loudoun Road arranging matters. If you wish to get into touch with him telephone Maida Vale 3003, or during the night at his home, 165a, Adelaide Road, N.W.3., telephone Primrose 5916.

It is advisable for boys to take to Scotland:

         1 thick rug or 2 blankets
         2 sheets
         2 towels.

             A. M. HANSON,

             GEORGE M. SMART.

5th September, 1939.

ARNOLD HOUSE SCHOOL.
       shall
   I----- be sending my boy to join
        not
the 7.40 train from Euston
-------------------------------- on Tuesday,
  8.41 train from Bletchley
September 19th.

       Signature . . . .
Please strike out the words not appropriate
and reply without delay.

Letter and reply card of 5th September 1939, detailing plans for evacuation to Edzell

class in which we were taught to produce long scarves for the servicemen's comfort. We all stuck to it as we were rewarded with a chocolate biscuit (scarce at the time) from a large tin.' Terence Cashmore remembered breakfasts of porridge with Scottish baps, long walks up the glen and playing amid the ruins of the old castle.

This was the time of the phoney war. The first air raids over London did not begin until May 1940. Some parents were irritated that their sons were being educated in inadequate conditions many hours away from their homes. A number withdrew their sons at the last minute, causing the School

financial difficulties. In October 1939 soundings were taken from parents. A circular was despatched under the names of both Miss Hanson and Mr Smart. 'We have heard from various sources that the arrangements made so hurriedly for the temporary education of the boys have not in many cases proved altogether satisfactory; and many parents have hinted that they would like their boys to return to us without further delay if only we were not so far away from London.' For boys who had already returned to London, the School re-opened at No. 3, Loudoun Road, in the mornings. The School also told parents that 'tuition of sisters could be arranged for' and a handful of girls attended Arnold House throughout the war. The last to be admitted was Susan Hunter in January 1944. This was as much to boost numbers as to be helpful to parents.

The despatch of young children across the ocean to North America continued until the tragic loss of life that followed the sinking of the SS *City of Benares* on 18 September 1940. Of the 407 passengers and crew, 260 lost their lives, including 77 of the 90 children on board. One of the survivors was 11-year-old Colin Ryder Richardson, who had joined Arnold House in 1936. He demonstrated remarkable calm

Tony Foxley, c. 1937

Transatlantic evacuees

Christmas cards to Miss Hanson at the end of 1939 showed that several boys had already been sent across the Atlantic by their parents for schooling in Canada as anxiety increased about the future of the war. Among them were the Paterson brothers, accompanied by their mother Dorothy, who wrote to Miss Hanson from Toronto in March 1940. Her letter concluded, 'On the whole, I think this was the right thing to do – it will always prove a good experience for the boys – they are safe, free from strain and splendidly fed. We are all wondering what Hitler and Mussolini are up to, meeting today at the Brunner Pass – things are obviously happening.' Miss Hanson wrote back, saying 'We have opened Number Three and it is not doing so badly, and if there are no air raids we certainly expect to double the numbers next term. People are coming back to Town.' This was

Three of the Paterson boys and Christmas cards from the family to Miss Hanson

true but short-lived; the Blitz would see the exodus renewed. Mrs Paterson may have been dismayed to read Miss Hanson's dismissive comments on the standard of education in North America – 'We have had a great many American and Canadian boys at Arnold House, and we have always found that their standard of education is considerably lower than ours – but then, very likely, in the Canadian schools they concentrate more on things that we do not take so much notice of.'

Colin Ryder Richardson (right) rescued from the SS *City of Benares*

in the face of danger when, waist-deep in water, he consoled and calmed an hysterical woman.

In February 1940 Miss Hanson and Mr Smart further revised the School's evacuation plans. They had been unable to convince some parents that rural Edzell was any safer than London. The report that bombs had been dropped over the Firth of Forth in October 1939 caused some anxious parents to speed northwards to bring back their sons, even though Edzell lay 80 miles to the north. George Smart in particular recognised the limitations of the Panmure Arms. Looking back many years later, he wrote, 'It would be idle to pretend that a hotel with other residents, however well disposed, makes an ideal place for a school. Not all the teaching staff were able to leave London and suddenly to turn dayboys of all ages, who have never been away from home before, into boarders presented other problems.'

Recognising the concern among some parents that Edzell was just too far away, Smart had arranged to transfer the boys who had been in Scotland to Northaw, his former school, in Kent. Mr Smart and Mr James, another member of staff, would accompany them. At the same time Miss Hanson expected both No. 1 and No. 3, Loudoun Road, to re-open for the Summer term in 1940.

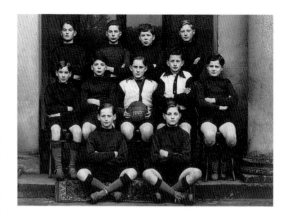

Arnold House and Northaw sports teams, Loton Park: Football, 1940, above left, and 1942 left. Cricket XI, 1941, above

Among the staff was George Smart's younger brother John, who himself had taught at Northaw before joining Arnold House at Edzell.

All these plans proved futile. German aircraft began swarming across the Channel. On 22 May Cecil Winter, Northaw's headmaster, wrote that

> it is very difficult to know exactly what steps to take for the best ... The general opinion seems to be that this actual part of the country, isolated and wooded as it is, with no military objective, is as safe as most places against aerial attack, and probably no more likely for parachute invasion than elsewhere, but much, of course, must depend on the turn of events abroad and, if the Germans reach the coast, I feel that many parents might think this likely to become a danger area ... In the meantime, we are considering the possibility of transferring the School to the West Country where we should hope to start again in the near future.

In fact the two schools moved to Shropshire just over two weeks later. Loton Park, the home of the Leighton family, was a 17th-century mansion set in 400 acres of parkland near the village of Alberbury nine miles west of Shrewsbury. Many large houses all over the country hosted evacuated schools, among them Chatsworth and Castle Howard.

The Arnold House boarders stayed at Loton Park almost until the end of the war. Hugo Langrish, the younger brother of Roger, was one of those who had not been allowed to join the School at Edzell. His family had taken a house on Exmoor but his education in the local village school was less than satisfactory. He pressed his mother to send him back to Arnold House as a boarder and reluctantly she conceded. Northaw boys, he found, were very different from Arnold House boys. Northaw, he remembered, was 'full of double-barrelled or Eton-bound gents'. Arnold House boys, in contrast, were typically from North London families whose wealth

was new rather than old money. Cecil Winter too was a contrast. He was, said Langrish, 'quite a frightening character, very much the opposite of George Smart, who was like an angel'. Many parts of the house, stuffed with historic artefacts, were out of bounds to the boys, but this simply posed them a challenge. Boys who could regale their peers with tales of exploring illegal places boosted their reputation – although sometimes they betrayed themselves by reappearing covered in dust. The magnificent grounds gave plenty of space for recreation and games although facilities for the latter were somewhat primitive. Langrish recalled one master giving a batsman guard on the cricket pitch as 'middle and cowpat'.

Terence Cashmore remembered an outbreak of measles, a serious affair when antibiotics were unheard of. The sick room was kept dark to protect the boys' eyesight and serious infection was treated with the sulpha drug M&B 693. 'At one time half the School was down with the disease which must have worried the staff and parents.' Food was ample, there was a large kitchen, and boys helped

Right: Loton Park, 1940

Arnold House and Northaw Schools, 1940
Fourth row: Lloyd-George, Holland, Whitby, Stapleton-Cotton I, Hardy, Porcelli, Brown, James, Campbell, Markham, Holder, Bowles, Nash I, Milburn, Smith I, Mackenzie-Low I, Houston, Wall, Dickinson, Gluckstein I
Third row: […], Oxborrow, Woolf, Stapleton-Cotton II, Lindesay-Bethune, Anson, Spier, Davis, Peters, Clough II, Lumsden II, Cashmore, Young
Second row: Foxley, Taylor, Webber, Ewen, Money, Rhodes, Connell, Colville, Lumsden I, Clough I, French, Sword, Reid
First row: Gracie, Smith II, Marsham, Heyward, Highwood, Nash II, Mackenzie-Low II, Saville, Hill, Beecham, Goodfellow, Gluckstein II, Stratton

A recollection of Loton Park

Colin Winser and his brother joined Loton Park in January 1942. Colin recalls:

> Lessons were held in the impressive hall wing, with the bottom form in the gallery, forms III and IV in the auditorium, form V on the stage and the Sixth Form quite properly in the adjoining green room. Simple arrangements, but somehow they worked. The original staff quarters above the hall, including a small chapel (which accommodated some eight Arnold House boys), acted as dormitories for some, while others used several of the many large bedrooms in the main part of the house. Inevitably, the plumbing arrangements were not up to the demands of such large numbers; there were few bathrooms or lavatories, so cubicles were erected in an outbuilding (probably stables or a cow shed) and chemical closets were installed – a chilly experience on morning parade in the depth of winter, which was a hard one in 1941–2.

The lack of heating and the restrictions of rationing (combined with appalling chilblains), together with the inevitable feeling of home sickness, made for a rather grim induction to life as a boarder.

Loton Park Grand Hall used as classrooms, 1940s

to pick the raspberries and gooseberries. 'Gooseberry fool and lashings of roast potatoes have stuck in my memory. Sweets and chocolates brought from home were impounded by the staff and handed out in very small doses until they were all gone.' Wood was collected from the deer park for the fires in the hall and throughout the house and boys were trained to use the cross-cut saw for cutting up the largest logs. In the autumn chestnuts were roasted on the hall fire.

Meanwhile, back in London, every effort was being made to continue the School in Loudoun Road. There was every reason for making the effort despite the onset of bombing raids. Many schools forced to close during the early days of the war never re-opened. A circular issued on 12 June 1940 announced that the School in Loudoun Road 'will remain open as long as it appears to be safe, and in the event of an air raid every possible care will be taken of the boys, though the parents must realise

Arnold House and Northaw Schools having a picnic and swimming in the Severn, 1940–1

From Miss Hanson and Mr. George Smart.

A R N O L D   H O U S E   S C H O O L
3 Loudoun Road
Saint John's Wood
N.W.8.

The School at Loudoun Road will remain open as
long as it appears to be safe, and in the event of an
air raid every possible care will be taken of the boys,
though the parents must realise that the ultimate
responsibility must rest with them.
There is a small underground air raid shelter at
Number One, and the School has permission to take the
remainder of the boys into the air raid shelter at the
Hospital of St. John and St. Elizabeth, the entrance to
which is exactly opposite the school garden gate in
Grove End Road.

12th June 1940

escape unscathed from German bombing. Many years later an Arnold House boy, James Fassam-Wright, discovered from his own research that an unexploded 50-pound bomb had fallen on the School playground on 12 September 1940. Between September 1940 and September 1942 just three boys, D. C. McKean, J. de Salis Winter and P. J. Tickell, are recorded as being admitted to Arnold House, joining the School at Loton Park. In the end it was Loton Park, rather than Loudoun Road, that kept Arnold House a living and breathing entity during the most difficult days of wartime.

Rowland Whitehead mentions another boy, Capidos, who came to the School around this time as a refugee from Greece following the Italian invasion in 1940, although his name does not appear in the records. He recounted how Capidos was introduced to the other boys at morning prayers.

that the ultimate responsibility must rest with them'. The School had its own small shelter and had also arranged to use the shelter at the Hospital of St John and St Elizabeth across the road. The garage at No. 3 was turned into a shelter. It was equipped with an escape hatch in case the main door became blocked. During raids boys would sit clutching a rope attached to the front wall by an iron ring, which they were instructed to pull in an emergency, when it would dislodge dry-mortared bricks and allow the boys to escape. Matters were further complicated by the requisition of No. 1, Loudoun Road by the Women's Auxiliary Air Force (WAAF), although the WAAF built a substantial air-raid shelter in the playground. Arrangements were made to use another large house elsewhere in St John's Wood for classes.

In fact wartime dislocation in the capital made it impossible to sustain the School in Loudoun Road, even though the premises were fortunate to

Above: Letter informing parents of air-raid precautions

Below: The escape hatch to the air-raid shelter, discovered during building work in 2000

Flying bombs

Colin Winser vividly recalled the explosion that made George Smart close the School in early June 1944. He and his brother had returned home for lunch, when

> I saw the doodle-bug (as they were soon named) flying straight towards us as I looked out of an upper window of our house in Queen's Grove, having failed to heed a call to come downstairs. My shouted warning and hasty descent coincided with the tell-tale sound of the engine cutting out, followed by a gentle rushing noise. Lying on the floor in a passage for shelter we held our breath and waited. Seconds later there was a mighty bang, the house shook and there followed the sound of shattering glass as the full impact of the blast wave was felt. We were unharmed and, finding that our house appeared to have suffered no damage although other buildings nearby did, we had lunch and, along with our neighbours (the Gilchrists), my brother and I set off for school again, only to be uncere-moniously sent packing from a closed establishment. The damage caused by the bomb was substantial, with the blast being strong enough to break windows up to half a mile away; even though the School buildings escaped unscathed, the Headmaster's nerves were in shreds. The School remained closed for the rest of the term.

A V-1 flying bomb, or doodle-bug

An almost emaciated, pale little new boy called Capidos, was asked by her to stand in front of us, and our parents, and tell us about his experiences … In a quavering voice he recounted the journey with his parents. He must have been terrified. At one point he faltered, near to tears, and began 'then we saw tanks …' when, quite overcome, he fainted and fell with a crash to the floor. Leaping to her feet the resourceful Miss Hanson cried 'Carry on singing!' and, with the piano thumping, we broke into 'Onward Christian soldiers, marching as to war'. Quite a good way to pull the show together.

The School re-opened in London after the worst of the bombing had ended, welcoming 29 new boys during 1942–3. But a new threat appeared in the summer of 1944, with the first flying bomb falling on London in June. By the end of July a million and a half people had left the capital. No sooner had the threat from flying bombs been overcome than the first rocket reached London in September. Between June 1944 and February 1945 these menaces killed nearly 9,000 Londoners. George Smart recalled that,

> Our only casualty was a boy who was slightly bruised when, with needless heroism, a mistress flung herself on top of him as a flying bomb cut out immediately overhead before exploding in Wellington Road. Latterly more time was spent in the shelter than in the School and fearing that the shelter would be struck while I was safely working in my study next door in No. 3 we closed Loudoun Road once more. This meant I could be with the boarders in Shropshire all the week instead of at weekends.

It re-opened yet again in September 1944. Among the boys was Cob Stenham, who had returned to England after leaving the School for evacuation first to Canada and then the West Indies. In the summer of 1945 Loton Park was returned to the Leighton family, the boys from Northaw and Arnold House departed and the government handed back No. 1, Loudoun Road. Arnold House returned home, welcoming boys old and new, but there would be no more boarders.

The Second World War claimed the lives of at least 53 former pupils and staff. Among them was Herbert Jacomb, attached to the RAF when he was shot down and killed over Belgium in May 1940. Richard Symes-Thompson was a doctor at St Luke's Hospital when he was wounded in one of the first raids of the Blitz in May 1941, dying later from his wounds. The young Sir Robert Peel was killed in action on board HMS *Tenedos*, sunk by the Japanese in Colombo harbour in Ceylon in 1942. Paul Davies-Colley was 23 years old when he was killed in action on Sicily in August 1943. Dimitri

Above: The altar cup and bowls dedicated to the memory of former pupils killed in the war

Right: The Second World War memorial in St Cyprian's

Below: The first Holy Book, marking those who died in the war with a small red cross

Galitzine, whose mother, Princess Marie Galitzine, had presented the prizes at Sports Day in 1927, was killed in action in Holland in October 1944. Miles Williamson-Noble survived the war only to be killed when the military aircraft in which he was travelling crash-landed on its approach to Oslo airfield in December 1945. Their example affected Miss Hanson just as much as the loss of former pupils in the previous war. As a memorial, the silver challenge cups competed for by boys between 1905 and 1930 were melted down and turned into communion plate. Two sets were made, with one chalice and patten donated to a church in the East End of London, and another to St Cyprian's. The first set has never been traced while the second was for a time lent to a former pupil, the Reverend David Paton, who returned it to the School in 2005. This set is now kept at St John's Wood Church and used for School services on occasions such as

Armistice Day. Those services also feature what are known in the School as 'The Holy Books', which record the names of every boy to have entered the School since 1905, marking those lost in action with a small red cross.

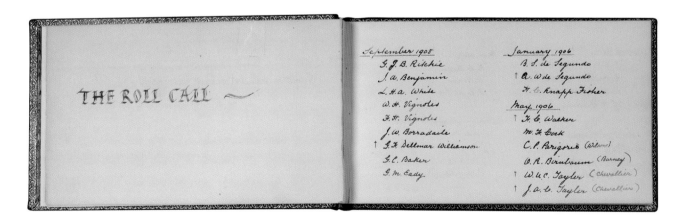

St David's Class including Edward Atkin, Michael Chamberlain, Leonard Davis, David Eaton, Alan Grainger, Leonard Petrie and William Stockler, 1952

'A New Chapter with a Fresh Look'
1945–66

O n the first morning of term in September 1945 the School welcomed 60 new boys. As George Smart remembered, 'It was difficult the first morning to establish the identity of five-year-olds, with unmarked pullovers, who only knew their fathers' Christian names. It was some comfort at the end of the day that mothers were equally at a loss to pick out their sons, in the glory of unaccustomed school uniform.'

This was the George Smart era. Miss Hanson made her last appearance at the School as a guest at the first post-war Prize Giving, held at the Seymour Hall in December 1946. The prizes were presented by one of her former pupils, Henry Brooke. The first Arnold House boy to become a member of parliament, Brooke later served as home secretary in Harold Macmillan's government. Miss Hanson died early in 1947, during one of the coldest winters on record. By then she was living with Miss Musson, who had been the School's matron before the war. She died a wealthy woman, leaving in excess of £145,000, worth several million pounds today. She made a number of generous bequests in her will, including a significant sum of money for his own use to George Smart 'as a token of my admiration of the way in which he has re-established my School known as Arnold House School which suffered so severely during the war'. She also left a further sum for Smart to establish scholarships for the sons of former pupils, particularly those who had lost their fathers on active service during the war. Miss Musson, Miss Hasencleaver and Miss Bretell were also benefi-ciaries as was the diocese of Sierra Leone. While she also left money to both the diocese of London and St Cyprian's, interestingly she also bequeathed a sum to the Catholic diocese of Westminster for eight annual masses to be said in perpetuity at the Church of Our Lady, St John's Wood, for 'the repose of the souls of William Montagu Hunt and the boys of Arnold House School'. This tradition is still maintained although the eight masses have been condensed into one.

George Smart was determined that the School's pre-war traditions and standards should be sustained. He brought a warmth to the School that impressed visitors and has remained an integral part of Arnold House. When the school inspectors arrived in 1954, they found 'a very pleasant community in which they were received in a courteous and friendly fashion by staff and boys alike. They left the School impressed with the devotion of the former and, speaking generally, with the capabilities of the latter.' The warmth Smart instilled helped to establish firm and long-lasting friendship with many boys after they left. Alan Lipscomb spent just 18 months at the School during the war but the Christmas cards his mother encouraged him to send to his former headmaster resulted in a lifelong friendship. Peter Rawlins, who left the School in 1964, recalled the support and advice Smart gave his mother when her husband died suddenly during Rawlins' first year at

senior school. Rawlins often had dinner with him and Smart wrote to him regularly in his elegant handwriting. For Rawlins, Arnold House was 'a family place. I felt comfortable there.' The staff were largely kind and caring and there was very little bullying or unpleasantness among the boys, who were encouraged to grow and develop and take up responsibility. All this, he believed, stemmed from the example set by George Smart.

It was helped by the continuity of staff, all of whom George Smart insisted, as had Miss Hanson, that the boys should address as 'Sir'. There was a handful of staff who had been at the School before the war. Until she retired in 1957 Miss Hasencleaver continued to inspire small boys with a love of mathematics while filling them with awe. Piers Plowright, who left the School in 1951, remembered how this tiny woman 'held classes in the palm of her hand, and inspired respect if not love'. Frank Smith had joined the staff in 1938, coming from more than a decade teaching at The Hall, the School's leading rival. Brisk and likeable, he also took games, often seemed to act as George Smart's deputy and retired in 1974.

Many of the teachers who joined after the war stayed at the School for at least five years. It is striking how many of them made such a deep impression on young boys that they could be recalled in detail decades later. One of the mistresses who struck a chord with many boys was Miss Spooner, just 22 years old when she joined the junior school in 1945. Nigel Southward entered the School at the same time and was among those who remembered that Pauline Spooner was 'simply the most attractive teacher you've ever seen'. Howard Raingold recalled that 'everyone was in love with Miss Spooner. She was very beautiful. She wore very expensive clothes and wore wonderful perfume.' A few years later John Smart, George's younger brother, also came to teach. He had a certain raffish air about him and was always a fund of good stories. He was,

Princess Marina, the Duchess of Kent, accompanied by George Smart (far right), meets Arnold House boys at the opening of the Princess Wing at the Hospital of St John & St Elizabeth, 1950s

in fact, a frustrated actor who had struggled for years to make a living on the boards, and spent part of his war service in the Entertainments National Service Association, or ENSA. One of the younger members of staff was John Robson, who came to the School in 1955. He had read French and German at King's College, Cambridge, before serving in the RAF during the war. A cultured man, always smartly dressed in blazer and flannels, he also helped to run games and, like John Smart, was popular with the boys.

Young boys were deadly in taking advantage of weaker masters. Mr Colquhoun, an Oxford graduate, taught French for several years immediately after the war. He favoured flowing scarves and wore a snap-brimmed trilby, teaching his subject with a beautiful accent, but his forte lay in giving additional teaching to boys on a one-to-one basis, whereas he found it impossible to keep order in the classroom. The boys in his class would use pens as peashooters, filled with damp blotting paper, and the room was littered by the end of the lesson. Piers Plowright remembered that Colquhoun's classes

would usually degenerate into paper and ink throwing ... every desk had a little white china inkwell placed in a hole on its sloping top and into which sputtering steel-tipped pens were dipped. The mess could be awful and the peculiar smell of dried ink that hung about your face, hair, suit, hands and even knees, is with me still.

There was a sense of devilment among small boys that sometimes got the better of those in charge of them. Ernest Gardner, who taught Latin and history from 1948 until 1969, had a quick temper that sometimes failed to hold his boys back. Howard Raingold remembered Gardner's vain attempts to recall a group of boys who had broken ranks on an outing to Primrose Hill. Baited by the

Classroom, 1940s. Front row, left to right: John Ungley, John Caulton, Gordon Rowland. Back row, left to right: Michael Wade, Tony Roques, Terry Grimes, with (in mirror) teacher Mr Colquhoun

jeering groups of boys from the nearby state school below them, they had charged down the hill, scattering their opponents. Gardner would reprove naughty boys in his Latin class with a quote many of them realised only much later came from *Macbeth* – 'The devil damn thee black, thou cream-faced loon!'

Pranks were part of schoolboy life. During one of the scripture lessons that began each day one boy placed a set of false teeth on the master's desk and then hid in the adjacent wall cupboard, timing his fall out of the cupboard flat onto the floor ten minutes into the lesson, causing predictable uproar. Peter Rawlins, returning to the School in 2012, pointed out that the studs on the banister of the main staircase in No. 1, Loudoun Road, were inserted following the attempt by his younger brother, Christopher, to slide all the way down. He failed, falling off half-way down, and breaking his leg.

None of this disturbed the essentially ordered nature of life at Arnold House. In an era when beating boys was still common at prep schools, discipline at Arnold House was gently administered. This did not mean the absence of corporal punishment. As Antony Japhet observed, 'You could not take many liberties at Arnold House.' Although the cane was never used, the gym shoe was occasionally applied on an errant boy's hand by Mr Smith. Some teachers developed an unerring accuracy with a piece of chalk and some boys felt a ruler across the back of their legs. Mrs Morton-Williams, recalled Piers Plowright, was a sweet and gentle woman unless boys in her English class became too boisterous. This would provoke her to 'line everybody up, get them to roll down their socks and then pass along the rear of the line, striking everybody once on their exposed calves'. But the view of the School commonly held by many boys was summed up by Adam Raphael, who was at Arnold House in the late 1940s – 'It was a good school because it had a caring atmosphere. There was no bullying, no browbeating; there were no threats. Individuals, even very obnoxious small boys, mattered.'

In an age when academic pressure was less intense, when the pursuit of results had not yet become feverish, when teacher training lacked consistency, the calibre of staff inevitably varied. Things were tolerated then that would never be permitted today. This applied as much to Arnold House as anywhere else. One elderly teacher without qualifications who joined the staff after the war was, remembered Tony Roques, 'rabidly anti-semitic, although nobody ever said anything'. On the other hand, the eccentricity of

Boys, 1940s

another elderly master belied his skill. There was a distracted air about Mr Castello, a tall, shambling figure whose clothes seemed slightly too large for him. He apologised to his class for his late arrival one morning with the excuse that his train had gone up the wrong tunnel. He would occasionally forget that he had left his

Bumpus Books on Oxford Street, from which Arnold House boys bought their books

lighted pipe in his jacket pocket and trail wisps of smoke around the classroom. But he was a formidable teacher of classics. Boys began learning Greek with him from the age of ten and their knowledge of Greek and Latin was well above average by the time they left the School. This standard was not confined to the classics. Many boys discovered that the teaching they received at Arnold House put them ahead of their peers on reaching public school. Peter Rawlins left for St Edward's, Oxford, in 1964, winning top 'O' level grades in English language, French, maths and Latin with very little work at the end of his first year. 'I had been educated to a standard at Arnold House that made it possible for me to sail through all my "O" level exams.'

Alistair Boyd, who spent two years at the School with his twin brother immediately after the war, recalled 'an extremely sympathetic and helpful bunch of teachers who no doubt reflected the benign yet inspiring leadership of the much loved George Smart'. But Smart did not tolerate sloppy teaching. Roger Langrish, who returned to teach at the School in 1946, remembered how Smart would not shirk from rebuking staff if he felt the School's position in the first rank of London prep schools was under threat. Boys were expected to work hard and without exception to pass Common Entrance; the question was which ones should be entered for scholarship examinations. On average between 1947 and 1966 the School recorded almost two scholarships every year.

School reports

George Smart personally corrected and approved every School report, often discussing them at length with each member of staff until late into the night. 'He could be waspish, openly and embarrassingly critical', recalled Roger Langrish, 'yet always ready to see the funny side. He could be wonderfully compassionate ... he could drive you up the wall but yet inspire loyalty and affection.'

School reports: Antony Japhet 1946, left, and Charles Rentoul, 1953, above

The inspectors on their visit to Arnold House in 1954 concluded that Smart knew his school well and was committed to 'seeking the best ways of developing it'. They observed that 'a characteristic of the staff in general is a whole-hearted attitude to their work ... The very few who are without recognised qualifications have a long experience of teaching; and, if there is no outstanding teacher, the general level of ability seems above the average for comparable schools.' In a curriculum typical of many prep schools they found that 'no subject to which much time is given is weak. A good standard is reached in classics, mathematics and French. In much of the English and in physical education there is teaching of unusual freshness and a marked quality of zest about the work.'

The School continued to be divided between the junior school, housed in No. 3, Loudoun Road, which accepted boys from the age of five, and the senior school, with Remove form acting as a bridge between them. In the senior school there were nine forms and the top three forms took lessons on Saturday mornings.

The School was developing a reputation for sending boys in particular to Westminster but this was just one among more than 20 public schools that accepted boys from Arnold House. A particular characteristic of the School during this period was that as many as 40 per cent of boys left at the age of eight for boarding prep schools. The decline in boarding would begin, and then only gradually, in the late 1960s. George Smart was never happy at losing boys to boarding schools before Common Entrance and usually insisted a boy would not be readmitted once he left. An exception was Howard Raingold, who had pestered his mother to send him to boarding school, only to discover it was a great mistake and he became desperately unhappy. His mother persuaded George Smart to allow Howard to return to Arnold House, helped in part because three of his brothers were still at the School, but

June 21st, 1954.   No. 2.

COMMON EXAMINATION FOR
ENTRANCE TO PUBLIC SCHOOLS.

LATIN.
PAPER A.

[60 *minutes*.]

I. Give the :—
Acc. Plur. and meanings of :—magister, homo, animal, gradus.
Gen. Sing. and meanings of :—miles alacer, senex idem.
1st Sing. Fut. Indic. Act. of :—tango, lavo, possum, fugio.
Latin for :—fifteen, no one, more wisely, whither ?
English for :—rogari, iam, sine auxilio, ullus.

II. Translate into English :—
1. Pater ejus equos in oppidum ducebat.
2. Imperator pontem nocte proxima facere statuit.
3. Dona talia nolite ad inimicos mittere.
4. Insula, quam vidimus, a litore non procul abest.
5. Statim ab urbe profecti cives pacem oraverunt.

III. Translate into Latin :—
1. Many boys were running out of the fields.
2. The king has given food to the slaves.
3. You said that you had left your sword in the camp.
4. The wind was so great that it drove the oxen into the sea.

IV. Translate into English :—
Hoc nuntiato dux omnibus equitibus imperavit ut suis succurrerent. Interim nostri tres horas fortissime pugnabant, et paucis vulneribus acceptis multos ex hostibus occiderunt. Postquam autem equites nostri in conspectum venerunt, hostes abjectis armis fugerunt, magnusque eorum numerus est interfectus.

Copyright reserved

The Latin Common Entrance exam paper, 1954

The junior school

The junior school is remembered fondly by many former pupils as a haven of gentleness. It was perhaps too much of a haven. In 1954 the inspectors remarked how the junior boys benefited from 'the kindly and conscientious supervision of all these [form] mistresses, although more could be done to stimulate self-reliance and independent study – so much is done for many of these boys, who are often brought to school by "nannies", as to give slight scope for developing self-reliance and initiative'.

The junior school, 1960–1

Howard never really felt that Smart forgave him for having left in the first place.

Boys entering Arnold House came from a broad range of backgrounds although most of them could be classed as coming from families that were comfortably off. Terry Grimes recalled that immediately after the war, 'there wasn't a lot of anything, and times were difficult for most people, although you later realised that the boys at Arnold House came from a privileged group, with fathers from professional backgrounds'. At one end of the spectrum there was Prince Muffakham Jah, grandson of the seventh Nizam of Hyderbad, one of the richest men in India, who arrived every morning in a chauffeur-driven Rolls-Royce. On the other hand, Terry Grimes remembered that it was not always easy for his parents to find the money for school fees (they were later delighted that he won a scholarship to St Paul's). Antony Japhet's father was a serving officer in India. 'What got me in,' he later recalled, 'was that my father was a lieutenant-colonel – rank helped.' The father of Tim Piper, who entered Arnold House in 1946, was a chartered accountant. William Falk's father was a local businessman who himself had been at the School in Miss Hanson's time. The parents of David Davies, admitted to the School in 1955, ran a grocery and sandwich shop near Euston station.

Peter Rawlins characterised the School in the late 1950s as being populated by the sons of 'the hard-working middle classes, an eclectic mob of relatively ordinary people'. Most of the boys lived close enough to the School to reach it either by walking (usually unaccompanied in those days

Prince Muffakham Jah, grandson of the seventh Nizam of Hyderbad (circled), 1949–50

when there was much less traffic), bus or a short tube ride. This was a time when the city was regularly afflicted by the dense choking smogs caused by the widespread use of coal in homes and factories. John Ungley, who joined Arnold House in 1945, remembered how visibility could be so limited that it was impossible to see from one street lamp to the next. But only once walking home from School did he get lost, when he crossed Marlborough Place diagonally rather than straight across, correcting his mistake by retracing his steps when he realised he was going uphill. The Clean Air Act of 1956 was prompted by the Great Smog of 1952 which killed 4,000 Londoners in just four days. At the Arnold House Prize Giving that year the smog seeped into the Seymour Hall, making it almost impossible to see from one end of the hall to the other.

Sport remained central to School life. Few former pupils of the period can recollect much in the way of other organised activities. For Antony Japhet, 'you came to learn, you did your lessons, and you went home with your homework'. Prep schools generally were only beginning to wake up to the importance of art and music by the late 1950s. At Arnold House music remained limited to

singing. Every class would perform a song at Prize Giving, such as the 'Skye Boat Song' or 'Here on the hills high hollyhocks hang'. Piers Plowright recollected that the occasion was 'merely a dreary procession of class-after-class singing exactly the same song', with boys unable to carry a tune reduced to mouthing the words. Music remained a Cinderella subject into the 1960s, as Peter Beckman, who left in 1968, remembered. Music, he said, was restricted to 'singing and triangles – I was hot on the triangle'. Yet John Tavener, who left in 1957 and would attain eminence as a composer, found joy in music at the School. He remembered with affection the singing teacher Miss Cain who broke his heart when she left for Canada; and he also had the chance to play the organ at St Cyprian's and the piano for assembly. But boys wanting to learn the piano did so outside School and it was not until the 1970s that Mrs Elizabeth Diack began teaching boys piano in School.

Drama was largely informal. Tim Piper remembered every Spring term each form putting on short plays or sketches on a makeshift stage in the main assembly room in No. 1, Loudoun Road. Terry Grimes once borrowed his father's ancient morning suit to play a waiter, annoying him by

Opposite: Right to left: Ian Buckley Sharpe, Terry Grimes, Mischah Scorer and John Ungley, 1940s

tearing a sleeve. There were entertainments when boys had the opportunity to demonstrate acquired skills such as conjuring. Adam Raphael recalled one star among the boys just after the war. He remembered 'one wet summer's day when the cricket had been cancelled being entertained by a small red-headed boy who could do the most amazing whistles. Train whistles, dog whistles, football whistles – and even odder noises like a cow being milked and an elephant giving birth. He was a brilliant comedian and had us all in fits of laughter. The small boy's name was Jonathan Miller.' Piers Plowright recalled how on wet games days Miller would perform brilliant impressions of trains in front of the other boys gathered in the bow-windowed classroom on the first floor. Alistair Boyd remembered Miller entertaining them with his impression of Danny Kaye in the recently released movie of *The Secret Life of Walter Mitty*. Miller would later hone his talents with the Cambridge Footlights at university and become well known as a raconteur in a distinguished career that embraced acting, directing and writing.

There were occasional visits to museums and galleries in central London. Occasionally a master might take a party of boys for tea to Fortnum & Mason and in 1948 a group was taken to Wembley Stadium for the London Olympics. The boys also walked in crocodile to St Cyprian's for services at the beginning and end of each term. Tony Roques recalled the vicar, Father Robson, coming to Arnold House for the service held on the feast day of the School's patron saint, St Michael. The boys remembered him because he whistled through his teeth, particularly with the word 'boys', which tended to come out as 'boyssshhh'. Although the strong contingent of Jewish boys could be excused from attendance, most of them went along and Howard Raingold was among those who fell in love with the hymns that were sung. Daily assembly was held in the large classroom in No. 1, Loudoun Road, when

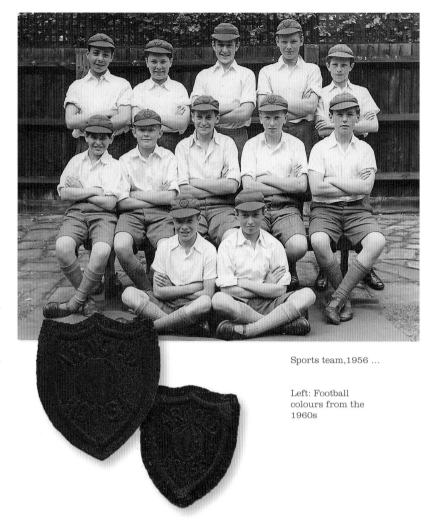

Sports team, 1956 ...

Left: Football colours from the 1960s

important announcements, such as the news of the death of the King in 1952, were made.

Assemblies were also the occasion when the detailed and unvarnished match reports compiled by Frank Smith and others were read out. One of the earliest surviving post-war reports was for a football match against Eaton House on 26 October 1948:

For some time past an Arnold House search for victory on the football field has seemed about as hopeless a task as the alchemist's attempt to unearth the philosopher's stone. One began to think that the only chance of success would be to send a challenge to some celebrities housed in Madame Tussaud's! Even then a result might have been a goal-less draw as Arnold House could have been frozen to complete immobility at the sight of some of the members of the Chamber of

... and 1964

The Deen Welter-Weight Boxing Trophy. First awarded in 1952 to John H. Deen

Horrors. Fortunately – or unfortunately – we have been spared this experiment by yesterday's victory against Eaton House.

Arnold House won 5–1. The School had been using playing fields at Canons Park in Edgware since the early 1950s and when the 2nd XI played cricket there against St Anthony's in July 1956 it was recorded that, 'The afternoon's play can hardly deserve the title of good cricket, for the St Anthony's Eleven were too weak to put up any serious resistance whilst the Arnold House players stuck rigidly to their motto of "slog or miss"'. When the football team thrashed Eaton House 6–0 at Canons Park in November 1957, the report observed,

> To call this an easy victory is to invite the comment that it could have been easier for the team showed only spasmodic periods of good play. During the first half in particular, the forwards tended to be too slow in getting on to the ball. Passing was weak on many occasions throughout the game, and the backs seemed incapable of clearing the ball far enough from the goal to eliminate danger. The halves often left too great a gap in the middle of the field, an

opportunity of which stronger opposition would have taken fuller advantage.

The report continued, 'After this welter of criticism, it would be as well to mention how we scored any goals at all'. Gerald Raingold, one of four brothers who attended the School, was a keen footballer who became part of a successful first team in the early 1950s. Dropped on one occasion, he was so determined to win back his place that, playing for the 2nd XI against Westminster Under School, he scored five of the team's seven goals in a match-winning display. Sadly, the match report does not appear to have survived.

Although boxing was supposed to be optional, almost every boy in the senior school took part. The School held a boxing tournament in the Seymour Hall every Easter term and a boxing exhibition always followed Prize Giving. Jack Gutteridge and

Canons Park

Canons Park was used for games every Tuesday and Thursday afternoon. In 1954 the inspectors had reported that 'a fine games field with a good pavilion is rented for the use of the older boys and the masters devote much time to coaching with obvious success'. Frank Smith, recalled Tim Piper, was 'a wonderfully typical prep school sports master who engendered fierce loyalty among the boys'. With George Smart, he accompanied the boys when they travelled by tube to Canons Park. Boys could also take the bus. There was one year when for some reason matches were also played at the grounds of the Indian Gymkhana Club at Osterley, reached by a coach hired from the local operator, Rickards. Junior boys were taken by coach to Hampstead Heath for football. As a relatively small school, Arnold House had many fewer teams or matches than in later years, but, said Peter Beckman, who entered the School in 1960, 'we were competitive'. Canons Park was also used to host the annual Sports Day, always accompanied by a cream tea. It was, remembered Beckman, 'a very grand affair. You did not see parents in casual clothes. They would mostly be in suits and dresses.'

Sports Day, Canons Park, late 1960s, with John Pepys (far left)

his twin brother Dick had been the boxing instructors at Arnold House since 1934. The family had long links with boxing and the twins were regarded as the best trainers in the country during the 1920s and 1930s.

In 1948 Jack Gutteridge handed over to his 22-year-old son, also known as Jack. Jack junior's cousin Reg became a well-known boxing journalist, writer and commentator. Under the name Jackie 'Mr TV' Pallo, Jack himself would earn fame as one of the two best-known wrestlers in the country, the other being Mick McManus, when the sport was at the height of its popularity on television during the 1960s and 1970s. Some boys – including Peter Rawlins who hated the regular humiliation in the

annual competition in front of parents – loathed the sport but others enjoyed sparring. Boxing was growing in popularity, catching the public imagination in the years after the war with the exploits of boxers like Freddie Mills, Randolph Turpin, Brian London and Henry Cooper.

John Ungley, who boxed in the 1940s, recalled that it was always conducted on a fairly friendly basis and there was an understanding that no boy would hit another too hard. Peter Beckman, boxing in the 1960s, remembered that it was never vicious – 'it was not a thing where you were trying to destroy the other boy' – and you were encouraged beforehand to take things easy if you were matched with a weaker opponent. Although Ungley never

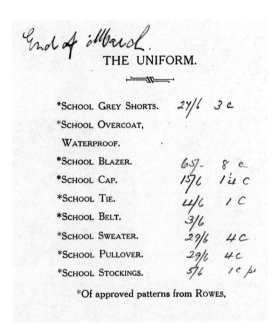

End of March.

THE UNIFORM.

*School Grey Shorts.   27/6   3 c

*School Overcoat,

   Waterproof.

*School Blazer.   65/-   8 c

*School Cap.   15/6   1¼ c

*School Tie.   4/6   1 c

*School Belt.   3/6

*School Sweater.   29/6   4 c

*School Pullover.   29/6   4 c

*School Stockings.   5/6   1 c p

*Of approved patterns from Rowes,

relished boxing, he found it stood him in good stead on the one occasion he was bullied. Taking his mother's advice, he put an end to the bullying by punching the bully on the nose. Gerald Raingold won the boxing tournament in his last year, knocking out in the semi-final Leonard Petrie, who would later become his brother-in-law, while his future wife and mother-in-law looked on. Winning the final, he took home a cup 'which was nearly as big as me'. Peter Beckman remembered that the old brown boxing gloves used by the boys 'were stuffed with horsehair and were coming apart at the seams and had a curious smell about them'. Jack Gutteridge, he recollected, would sing 'Blood! Blood! Glorious Blood!' to the tune of the Flanders and Swann hit song, 'Mud! Mud! Glorious Mud!' Beckman enjoyed the sport, later becoming one of the last heavyweight champions at Harrow.

Alongside cricket, football, boxing and annual athletics there was also swimming. Instruction took place during the Summer term, firstly in the Hampstead Baths along the Finchley Road, with their overpowering smell of chlorine and damp coconut matting, and later in the new baths opened in 1964 at Swiss Cottage. An annual gala was held in the baths at the Seymour Hall.

On days when games were cancelled, in addition to indoor entertainments when it was wet, the boys had the chance to play games like cops and robbers in the sandhills on the Hampstead Heath Extension. Tim Piper recalled the excitement one day when a boy lost his shoe in the bog and had to be taken home by taxi.

Red distinguished the Arnold House boy on and off the playing field. The football strip consisted of blue shorts and red tops. The carnation-red blazer was the main component of the School uniform. As a rule, every boy was expected to wear shorts. There were exceptions among those boys who were so tall that they looked ridiculous in shorts. After the war, when rationing was still in place, it was usual, observed Antony Japhet, for boys to join Arnold House wearing a blazer much too large and leave in one that was much too small. The big disadvantage of the red blazer was that it easily identified any Arnold House boy up to mischief out of School. It also made them a magnet for the boys from the local state school, although confrontations between the two sides never amounted to much more than ridicule.

While it was easy for some boys to travel home for lunch, many took their meal at School. Straight after the war, Miss Beauchamp, the School housekeeper until 1969, made the most of rationed resources, although few boys appreciated it. Things had improved by the mid-1960s. 'I loved the food, I really did,' recalled Peter Beckman. 'We got the best chocolate pudding and chocolate sauce [which] I've never been able to match again.' Lunch was taken formally, with the boys sitting in forms at tables headed by members of staff, and they were expected to take time after the meal to allow their food to settle. Milk and biscuits were provided every morning break.

The School buildings changed scarcely at all during this period. There was always enough space both inside and out for the number of boys. There was little competition between schools, and marketing was almost unheard of. The idea that one improved physical facilities to attract potential parents to the School would never have occurred to George Smart or his peers at other schools. In any case few parents were interested in comparing Arnold House with other prep schools. They applied to send their sons to Arnold House on recommendation. With the post-war bulge in the birth-rate, there was never any shortage of applicants. Parents accepted that any communication they had with the School would be distant and infrequent, limited to the termly report, a formal notice concerning important dates and the occasional letter advising a rise in fees. Otherwise they would be summoned only when something was amiss. Antony Japhet remembered how his

parents were invited into School to be told how horrified the Headmaster was about Antony's poor examination results in the term before he sat Common Entrance. It was the stimulus he needed to improve, pass Common Entrance and win his place at public school.

These and other limitations did not diminish the happy atmosphere of Arnold House. It would be safe to say that most boys left the School with fond memories. Many of them looked back on their time at Arnold House as much happier than the years they spent at public school. Many friendships formed at that tender age lasted for life. William Falk believed that 'friendship was by far the most important thing I've taken away from Arnold House'. Howard Raingold 'loved Arnold House. After I left I came back far too often and George Smart eventually told me I had to stop. They were happy, happy, happy days. George created a really happy school with really happy boys.' The kindness and care shown by so many staff helped to establish excellent relationships with the boys. For Tim Piper, 'they were happy times and boys had an affection for the School'. In looking back, he believed that 'the School instilled a sense of responsibility and purpose ... it gave you a feeling you were going to get on in the world. Arnold House really set you up for life.' Peter Rawlins shared this view that the School encouraged young boys to develop and take up responsibility. This, Rawlins believed, was part of the purpose of the prefect system. He remembered as head boy supervising play and mealtimes, keeping an eye on junior boys and 'quietly encouraging mothers away from the School while prising small boys from their mothers' knees'.

The affection felt by so many boys for the School inspired George Smart to encourage more formal links between Arnold House and former pupils. On the occasion of the School's golden jubilee in 1955 he hosted a dinner at the Trocadero in Shaftesbury Avenue. The encouragement he gave

A presentation from the boys in 1955 to George Smart on the School's golden jubilee

those in attendance would lead to the formation two years later of the '42 Club, a name arising from the decision to limit membership to those who had been at the School since its re-opening in London in September 1942. The Club quickly became an established part of the School, holding annual dinners from 1957 onwards. Other social and sporting events have been organised and the Club has presented prizes, gifts and ties for boys leaving the School.

George Smart celebrated his 60th birthday in 1965. He had reached the same crossroads that had

prompted Miss Hanson to pass on ownership of the School. He too needed to think about the future of the institution that he had owned, managed and part-funded for nearly 30 years. There was no question that Arnold House, based on its past achievements, had a future. Selling the School was probably dismissed pretty quickly as an option. Firstly it was not in George's nature to hand over his life's work to someone else. Secondly things had changed in the prep-school world. Criticism in the Fleming report published in 1944 of private profit in prep schools had stimulated a move to turn many of them into charities. By 1965 more than a fifth of existing prep schools had become charities, a trend that accelerated, with three-quarters of IAPS schools ceasing to be privately owned by 1981. It was this path that George Smart decided to adopt for Arnold House. His application for the School to become a charitable educational trust was approved by the Department for Education and Science in the autumn of 1966 and on 11 October Arnold House School Limited was established as a company limited by guarantee. There were seven subscribers. Two were heads of senior schools fed by Arnold House, David Black-Hawkins of UCS and J. D. Carleton of Westminster. The remaining five were Smart's friends James Livingstone, Sir James Waterlow and Raymond Willis, former parent Peter Sebastian and former pupil Colin Winser. They formed the first board of governors under the chairmanship of Peter Sebastian, with the addition of another former pupil, Tony Roques. While George Smart also sat alongside them as a Life Governor, he remained as Headmaster. The next decision was to choose who would succeed him to lead Arnold House.

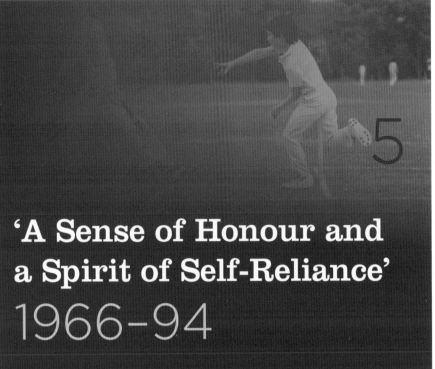

'A Sense of Honour and a Spirit of Self-Reliance'
1966-94

Arnold House boys meet Diana, Princess of Wales during a visit to the St John's Hospice, 1986

O ver 60 years Arnold House had reflected the forceful personalities of its two proprietors, Amy Hanson and George Smart. As owners, they had been in a singular position, accountable to no one other than themselves. They had complete liberty to mould the School as they thought fit. With the transition of the School from a privately owned institution into a charitable educational trust, this had to change. The Headmaster was now accountable to the governors, who were collectively responsible for the School. Such a change in culture would not occur overnight. Although George Smart's decision was made with the interests of the future of the School at heart, it did nothing to diminish his considerable influence. He remained Headmaster and sat as Life Governor on a board of governors hand-picked from close acquaintances who held him in deep respect. It cannot have been an easy situation either for George Smart or for the new governors although it was not unusual. The histories of many schools

yield instances where the continuing presence of a long-established previous head overshadowed his or her successor.

Appointing someone to take over from George Smart, as Colin Winser later observed, 'understandably proved more difficult than expected in view of the personality of the incumbent and the absence of any accommodation for an appointee, who at that stage was not going to receive a high salary'. In September 1967 John Pepys took up the post of deputy headmaster with a view to succeeding George Smart on the latter's eventual retirement. Educated at Sherborne and Oxford, John Pepys had had a long and distinguished teaching career. In 1946 he was appointed head of Colet Court School in London, where he spent nine years before leaving to head St Peter's School at Pointe-à-Pierre in Trinidad, originally established by the American oil giant Texaco. He accepted the post at Arnold House on his return from abroad. In September 1968 it was announced that Pepys would take over from George Smart as Headmaster in April 1969. Smart told parents that Pepys 'will bring to [the School]

new ideas and a fresh outlook'. But he also added, 'I am a Life Governor of the School and I should like you to know that my interest in it will be no less after my retirement'.

Whatever the aspirations of John Pepys, his time at Arnold House is cast in the shadows thrown by the continuing influence of George Smart, not least through a hand-picked board of governors still grappling with their role. Pepys's own career was coming to an end and his was a stop-gap appointment. He may have wished to bring 'new ideas' to Arnold House but he was faced not only with George Smart but also the almost empty coffers of the School, a situation the governors were striving to remedy by raising fees to make them comparable with local competitors and to counter the adverse impact of inflation. Pepys was a self-effacing man. Somewhat aloof, self-contained and very correct, he spoke quietly and gently. One boy, Eddie Villiers, remembered that Pepys moved around the School so silently that he became known as the 'Grey Ghost'. Another, Robert Max, later recorded that he appeared to be 'a saintly man who never raised his voice'. Others, like Anastassis Fafalios, Edward Brett and Charles Falk, found their Headmaster reserved and proper, a stickler for making sure that the boys looked neat and tidy. He could be acerbic but he was a likeable man with a dry sense of humour. One member of staff, Diccon Swan, who was teaching English, described him as 'a tall, lean, elegant man with the look of an eagle: he had slightly hunched shoulders and his head could jut forward so that his searching eyes, swept-back hair and trimmed eyebrows could scrutinise you piercingly'. Despite his distance, he had the interests of the boys at heart, as one might imagine of a man who had been appointed to

THE
CARGILL BOWL

THE
PAM CUP
1926

Three School trophies. Left to right: The Pam Cup, goes to the best all-rounder in Under-11 cricket; the Cargill Bowl, received by head boys; the Forbes Trophy, awarded for English Literature

his third headship. Eddie Villiers followed the family tradition by leaving Arnold House for Eton but he hated it. His mother called John Pepys who within a short time returned her call to say he had found a place for her son at Highgate School. Courteous and diplomatic, he was adept at dealing with difficult situations, and he gained the respect of many parents during his time as head.

Faced with all the constraints outlined above, it is unsurprising that Pepys was unable to bring much change to the School during his eight years as head. It is difficult to spot any difference between the prospectus produced at the end of the 1960s and its predecessors. The number of boys, aged from five to 14, with around 150 seniors and 50 juniors, was much the same as it had been in the early 1950s. The structure of the School was the same; while it was recognised that some boys were not academically inclined, little support was provided. There was scant knowledge of learning difficulties such as dyslexia but this was typical of most schools at the time. Activities were still limited. A handful of visits were

organised to the major museums and galleries. Sport was dominant. Juniors still played on Hampstead Heath before travelling to Canons Park from the age of eight. Games afternoons were still every Tuesday and Thursday.

Eddie Villiers remembered how the boys would begin changing on the bus to Canons Park as soon as it turned left by the Blue Star garage. Match reports were still read out at assembly where colours were also awarded. Each boy who achieved three wickets in an over or scored 50 runs in a match received a brand new cricket ball. Boxing was still important, taken up at the age of seven or eight, and the annual tournament remained a central event in the School calendar. Jack Gutteridge, alias Jackie Pallo, was still the instructor. 'There you were,' recalled Graham Jacobs, a contemporary of Eddie Villiers, 'with blood pouring out of your nose, and Jackie Pallo shouting in his Cockney accent, "Come on, son! Raise your 'and!"' Pallo, loud, lively and different, once brought with him to the School his friend Terry Spinks, the Olympic boxing gold medallist and world champion. Eddie Villiers relished boxing – 'until I got a bit bigger – or until the boys I fought caught up with me – and it began to hurt'.

At the annual swimming gala a table draped in the Union Jack and covered in trophies was set up beside the pool for the presentation of prizes to shivering boys. At Sports Day too, Eddie Villiers recalled, 'there were cups for everything'. He and his brother won a bagful of cups one year which proved costly for his parents who had to bear the cost of the engraving. Boys were permitted to take home the cups they won for 12 months.

Music was making some progress if only slowly. The School's first music director was appointed in 1972, stimulating instrumental tuition and the beginnings of a School orchestra. Piano lessons had already been introduced. In 1975–6 the opening across the road of the American School with its own theatre enabled Diccon Swan to direct the School's first full-scale production, the musical *Oliver!* Swan played Fagin, with another staff member, Carol Watson, as Nancy, and Christopher Cooper and Maxwell Burke as Oliver and the Artful Dodger respectively. For many years the only drama had been the annual poetry competition which put off as many boys as it encouraged.

Food was indifferent. Anastassis Fafalios recalled how ice cream seemed always to be served on the coldest days in the year while the best food was dished up on games days when no one could do it justice. Graham Jacobs listed a staple lunchtime diet of roast beef, fish fingers, shepherd's pie, sausages and stews, accompanied by potatoes, cabbage and peas. Custard seemed to come with everything. Chocolate pudding with chocolate custard remained the dream dessert.

Looking back, Robert Max described Arnold House as a school run on conservative and traditional lines. Public events were very formal. Prize Giving, still held at the Seymour Hall, was 'a

Staff. Ms Smith, Ms Watson and Mrs Cantor, 1975

Mrs Morgan and Mr Williams

Mr Everett

remarkably intimidating affair with long speeches ... we had to sit in complete silence upstairs for hours and hours waiting to be presented with whatever honour we had earned because the slightest sound reverberated through the whole building'. For Edward Brett, who joined the School in 1975, it was an old-fashioned and austere place.

Yet the stasis in which the School found itself also ensured its values were unchanged. As the prospectus stated, 'the School tries to foster a sense

Boys, 1970s. Back row, left to right: Simon Taylor, Adam Wilcox, Jonathan Green, Nicky Martin, Mark Layton. Front, kneeling: Andrew Ruhemann

Anastassis Fafalios

Christopher Owen

Timothy Sutherland Smith

of honour and a spirit of self-reliance, of cheerfulness and self-discipline'. In 1975 the school inspectors, making their first visit since 1954, found the boys were 'lively, endowed with ability and enthusiasm'. Since boys were expected to take Common Entrance in their stride, there was little academic pressure on any of them. Arnold House remained a happy place. There was an evident tolerance among the boys. Edward Brett recalled one boy who suffered from a form of cerebral palsy but other boys thought nothing of it and accepted him for who he was. The junior school was still a haven for young boys. The mistresses in charge of its four forms, observed one school inspection report, 'provide a kindly, sympathetic and encouraging atmosphere for the younger pupils'. Edward Brett remembered beginning in St Patrick under Miss Brookhouse who corralled naughty boys in the playpen; and singing 'Bananas in Pyjamas' with Mr Gibbon, the music teacher, with half the boys

who had not yet learned the words gnashing their teeth and miming instead.

Little boys formed their own gangs, made up their own language ('Eee! Melly!' was apparently a popular exclamation) and developed long-lasting friendships. When Graham Jacobs left in 1975, 'I was terribly upset and I remember crying profusely'. But he moved on to his senior school at Highgate accompanied by several of the close friends he had made at Arnold House. Among them was Eddie Villiers, who reflected that 'the great thing about the School was that it was a place where you made really good friends'. Long-serving staff, like the well-respected John Robson, provided continuity. The departure of a stalwart like Frank Smith, recollected Graham Jacobs, who entered the School in 1968, had 'half the School in tears'. The Miss Spooner of an earlier generation gave way to the Mrs Dunant of the late 1960s. 'We all liked her,' recalled Anastassis Fafalios, 'because she wore a

The School and boys
in the early 1970s

Science Lab, 1975, with Mr Ramel

its premises particular attention might be given to the needs of physical education, music, art and craft, the library and dining. Additional space would enable the School to develop a more flexible and varied programme.'

Lack of space was one reason for what the inspectors regarded as the haphazard organisation of the senior school (they were much happier with the way the junior school was run). This was compounded by a disruptive system of promotion between forms that destabilised the continuity of education for some boys. Lessons were also disrupted by too much time given to games and PE. While noting the development of science in the curriculum, a trend among prep schools since the late 1960s, remedying many years of neglect, and the addition of a small laboratory in 1968, the inspectors noted that 'drama is almost entirely neglected' and art and craft deserved more time. The inspectors were also concerned about the high turnover amongst staff, inconsistencies in standards of marking and presentation and the lack of any policies on teaching or curriculum development. There was not enough consultation between members of staff, and in emphasising the importance of staff meetings in remedying this deficiency the inspectors were making an implied criticism of the leadership of the Headmaster. There were distant echoes of comments made by inspectors many years before. The inspectors repeated the remarks of their predecessors that the junior school could do more to encourage greater self-reliance among younger boys, and that teaching was focused too rigidly on passing the Common Entrance, giving boys little encouragement to study for themselves.

John Pepys was dismayed by the report, rejecting some criticisms while observing that others were already being tackled. But his comments betray his frustration at the limitations placed on the development of the School by the lack of space and

mini-skirt and long boots!' Diccon Swan, who later became an accomplished painter, made English colourful and exciting. Staff in general, reported the inspectors in 1975, were 'enthusiastic and hard working' and classroom relationships were good, although boys who misbehaved still faced flying chalk in the classroom.

While the school inspectors had many warm things to say about Arnold House in 1975, their report highlighted the School's weaknesses. Although not overcrowded, the School, they said, was full and the available space could be better used. Sanitary accommodation needed upgrading (and the practice of boys using their own towels should be given up in favour of using disposable towels). The library was too small, poorly organised, rarely open and had too many out-of-date books. For PE there was insufficient equipment and the practice of doubling up classes made proper supervision impossible. While resources and facilities were generally adequate, the inspectors believed that 'if the School were able, in the long term, to enlarge

The whole School, 1977

resources. 'I agree that more WCs and basins would be desirable but where are they to be?' An art room would be welcome 'but where? Where is alternative provision to be made for cloak rooms? And for sports equipment? I agree there should be more space for PE, music, art and craft, the library and dining, but short of rebuilding, I cannot see how it is to be achieved.' Time after time Pepys returns to this theme – for instance, dedicated subject classrooms would be ideal, 'but the building is not really conducive to boys moving about the School from room to room'; or 'A proper Art Room is definitely needed'; or 'A proper Music Room is also

needed'; or 'The provision of additional space would, of course, make all the difference to the work of the School'.

It was not an easy time for those running the School. There was no shortage of demand for places since the School retained its reputation as one of the leading prep schools north of the Thames. The School needed to continue to develop – in fact, such development was overdue – but was facing the consequences of George Smart's minimal interest in the School's financial position, coupled with an inflation rate that peaked at 25 per cent in 1975.

John Pepys retired at short notice in 1977 through ill health. At the end of his last term in the summer of 1977, with the whole School assembled in the playground, Pepys came out onto the fire escape, a whistle was blown and each class formed into a series of letters spelling out 'Goodbye', raising a gentle smile on the face of the departing Headmaster.

One governor, Colin Winser, recollected how the search for Pepys' successor 'produced a collection of rather uninspiring applicants until one man, who had withdrawn his application for personal reasons, resubmitted it several months later and clearly provided the type of approach to prep-school head-mastering that the School needed'. Another governor, Alan Lipscomb, was also convinced that this was the outstanding applicant for the post. Some governors had doubts, not because of the applicant's approach to the School or his views on education, but rather because he had recently been divorced and remarried. Their doubts were over-come and the appointment was made.

The fourth Headmaster of Arnold House was the 47-year-old Jonathan Clegg, popularly known as 'Johnny'. Born in Manchester, he himself was educated at a small boys' prep school, Charney

Hall, in Grange-over-Sands, about which he had nothing but fond memories. Charney Hall closed sometime after the early 1970s and the site was redeveloped for housing. Clegg moved on to Shrewsbury, studied law at Oxford and completed his national service in the RAF. At Oxford he gained a blue for football. He had had trials for Manchester United and was offered professional terms by Wolverhampton Wanderers but in those far-off times professional football was not as lucrative as teaching. In 1954 he began his career at Holmwood School near Formby on Merseyside, another small boys' prep school that eventually closed in the late 1990s. He was appointed joint headmaster in 1959 and remained at the school until he moved to Arnold House in 1977.

Seeking a new start, he came to Arnold House with his second wife, Gilly, and their six children. Their partnership lit up the School and they became renowned for the generosity of their hospitality. But it took the couple time to settle in and they were faced with not a few challenges. The School had never provided separate accommodation for the head. When there were boarders Miss Hanson had lived in School. There was never any need for George Smart to do so and he was affluent enough to acquire his own property near the School. London property prices made that impossible for Johnny Clegg. The governors agreed to purchase a property and acquired a family house in Briardale Gardens close to the Heath. But it was not ready at the beginning of the Autumn term in 1977 and for the first half-term the family took a one-bedroom flat above a local fish and chip shop in Lisson Grove for which they paid the rent. Anxious about starting a new life in a part of the world with which he was not intimate, Clegg found that even as a new Headmaster his suggestions for change met with some resistance from a governing body on which George Smart was still the key influence. Correspondence shows that even in the

Johnny Clegg

early 1990s Smart was still taking a seigneurial attitude towards the School. Clegg came to hate attending governors' meetings, although he eventually developed a warmer relationship with both the governors and George Smart. For a man unused to having his decisions questioned, it also took time to adapt to the constant stream of parents coming to make their views known to him – Clegg was quite taken aback, for instance, when one father even suggested his own son would make the perfect head boy.

But it turned out that there were good reasons why many parents were queuing up to meet the new Headmaster. Clegg's wife Gilly later reflected that her husband had no idea how much he had taken on. When he made his first report to the governors in November 1977, he was apologetic for the criticism it contained. Exempt from his strictures was the junior school about which he had nothing but praise. He described it as 'without question the best department of its kind I have ever

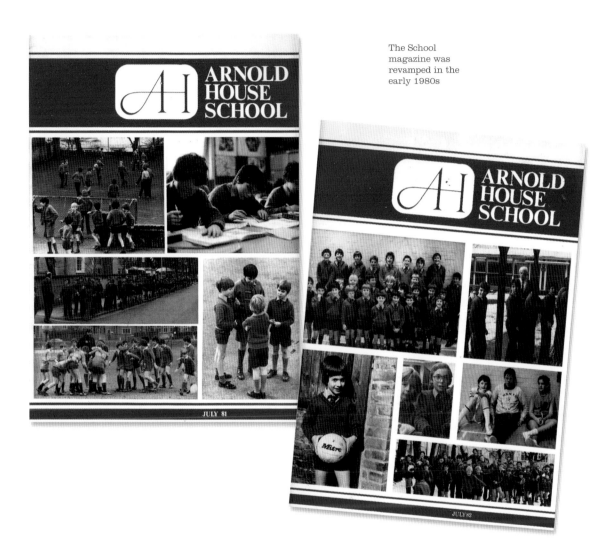

The School magazine was revamped in the early 1980s

met'. The staff under Miss Leon were a well-led and outstanding team. He was much less complimentary about the senior school. 'My overall impression', he remarked, 'was of an aged machine slowly grinding to a halt'.

Clegg's report gave the impression of a ship that had been drifting aimlessly. Some of what he had to say amplified comments made by the inspectors in 1975. The latter had obviously been diplomatic in the way they made their remarks about the lack of any strategy for developing the curriculum, the

variable standards of presentation and marking, the failure of staff to collaborate or communicate effectively with each other and the ineffective leadership of the School. Clegg could scarcely conceal his astonishment at the failure to devise a cohesive approach towards standards of work, the curriculum overall or individual subjects within it. He spelled out the result – 'By any standards, much of the work was totally unacceptable'. The good relationships in the classroom that had been a hallmark of the School appeared to be deteriorating.

There was a sense of detachment between pupils and teachers. Pupils lacked direction – 'whether it be in their work and their attitude to it, in their appearance, in their behaviour or in their manners' – and staff lacked leadership. Other comments in Clegg's report indicated that standards had clearly been slipping in the two years since the last inspection. The frustration expressed by John Pepys seems to have become a resigned indifference to his inability to change things as he neared retirement. Clegg pointed to the fact that about a quarter of all boys were having academic coaching outside School. This, he said, was 'an unnecessary and counter-productive situation as the boys come to believe they pass their exams regardless of what happens in school'. Coaching, however, would remain entrenched among successive generations of parents regardless of any academic improvements made by the School. The Headmaster reported that every parent he had seen had shared similar concerns – 'more than a few have been within a touch of moving their boys and all without fail have expressed support for a firmer line to be taken on all these aspects of School life'.

Action was already being taken. Clegg had outlined his approach separately to staff and pupils. He had found great support and enthusiasm among staff for his determination to put things right. The boys had been given a clear indication of what was expected of them and standards were already improving. Clegg was intent on making long-overdue changes. The dearth of extra-curricular activities related by boys of almost every generation would be rectified. There would be lunchtime and after-school clubs encompassing a range of interests. External visits would become a regular feature of School life. Visiting speakers would be invited to talk to the boys. It was time to communicate more openly and more comprehensively with parents. 'I believe', wrote Clegg, 'parents have a right to have as much information as

Johnny Clegg with Martin Goudie (left) and Alexander Gross (right), bridge club, c. 1986

possible provided for them to assess and understand their child's progress through school.' Every year a parents' evening for each form would be arranged. Reviewing the School timetable would enable better use to be made of the school day and create more time for music and art. The Headmaster's first report concluded by attempting to sweeten the bitterness of what had gone before – 'You have a wonderful school here ... the material is there to make Arnold House, I hope, the best by far of all London schools.'

Clegg maintained the School's traditional admissions policy. There was no competitive entry and the School continued to welcome boys of mixed ability, with the aim of encouraging each of them to reach their full potential without undue pressure. Certainly many boys at the School during this period do not recall any overt academic pressure. Charles Falk, who left in 1982, believed he was well taught. While his parents were worried that his apparent lack of effort would prevent him passing Common Entrance after receiving some adverse comments from staff at parents' evening, Johnny Clegg was always absolutely confident he would pass. And he did, securing a place at Harrow. For some boys pressure came through their parents, some of whom discouraged their sons from taking part in School productions during their Common Entrance year. Private coaching remained prevalent, regardless of what the Headmaster might say at parents' evenings. In the late 1980s there was some pressure from governors concerned that able boys were not being sufficiently stretched and Clegg suggested grouping together potential scholarship boys in a single form at the top of the senior school.

But the practice of extending school to every other Saturday morning for senior boys was discontinued in the early 1990s. To help parents and their sons in their choice of public school, Clegg introduced Leavers' Forums, when senior housemasters were invited to speak to parents. While Westminster was still a favourite destination for many boys, the list remained lengthy. In the 1980s, for instance, it also included Bradfield, Bryanston, City of London, Clifton, Eton, Haileybury, Harrow, Highgate, Marlborough, Merchant Taylors', Oundle, Rugby, St Paul's,

Computer technology, 1993

Sevenoaks, Stowe, Tonbridge and UCS. The Headmaster, unlike his immediate predecessors, made sure that he developed close links with heads and senior staff at many of the leading public schools. His extensive knowledge and the soundness of his advice on choosing the school most appropriate for each boy gained for him among parents the sobriquet of 'The Oracle'. By 1988 the Headmaster could report to the governors that 'applications were at a phenomenal level. There were even long waiting lists of parents wishing to view the School.'

They were attracted in part by the School's consistent success in Common Entrance, usually with every boy passing the examination. Common Entrance underwent considerable change during the 1980s, culminating in its biggest shake-up for some time when it was brought into line with the newly introduced National Curriculum at the end of the decade. This was the first time that Common Entrance had reflected the curriculum generally being taught across the country. Science had been the weak spot in the curriculum of many prep schools until the late 1960s. Arnold House was slow to catch up and it was only with the arrival of Johnny Clegg that science teaching was strengthened. Under a new science teacher, John Grey, a course was developed that equipped the boys with the foundations of biology, chemistry and physics. As one boy, Ed Sanders, remembered, 'we suddenly became aware that there was more than one branch of science'. The first extension to the School featured a better-equipped laboratory. In other subjects, such as Latin, boys still found not only that the standard of teaching at Arnold House exceeded the requirements of Common Entrance but that they were often years ahead of the teaching provided at their public schools. With the development of computer technology, computer lessons were added to a revised timetable in the early 1990s.

The School Song

Music by Denis King. Words by Joshua St Johnston.

Comitas et Industria

Verse 1 – Sung by all

School of study, school of work,
Where scholarship still finds
A love of Science and the Arts,
To open youthful minds.

Chorus – Sung by all
Courtesy and industry
Give Arnold House its name.
Boys who practise both of these
Bring Arnold House to fame.

Verse 2 – Sung by all

School of comradeship in sport,
Where games are played with zest,
In winter, summer, win or lose,
Our teams will give their best.

Chorus – Sung by all

Verse 3 – Choir only

School of charity and help
To all in word and deed,
For we, who have so much in life,
Must comfort those in need.

Verse 4 – Sung by all

School of friendship, school of fun,
Where constant humour cheers.
Our loyalty to Arnold House
Will strengthen with the years.

Chorus – Sung by all

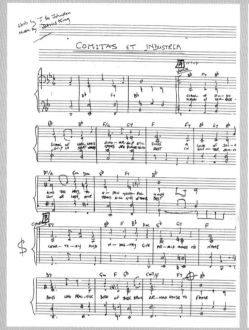

The manuscript of the School Song,
Comitas et Industria, 1983

Clegg was particularly eager to see the integration of the arts within the School curriculum. Teresa Burman was appointed director of music, remaining until her retirement in 1995. Enthusiastic and inspiring, she was regarded by the boys with affection. One year as a birthday celebration her husband arranged for the choir to visit her house and sing 'Happy Birthday' – although they had to wait for her to return from a shopping trip. She was just the sort of person Johnny Clegg wanted to lift the School's musical life when facilities remained primitive. She made the most of being able to play the guitar, moving around the form rooms. As the School magazine later recorded, she was 'taking her lesson with her, cassette recorder in one hand and guitar in the other'. Edward Brett

Teresa Burman
teaching flute

Lesley Ralphs, head of art, 1982–2005

recalled how she loved teaching the boys the songs of Andrew Lloyd Webber and took a group of them to a performance of *Joseph and the Amazing Technicolor Dreamcoat*. Boys also went carol singing to old people's homes, with Mrs Burman accompanying them on her guitar. She organised concerts in the American School, at one of which, in 1983, a new School song, *Comitas et Industria*, was performed, with music by Denis King and words by Joshua St Johnston.

All this was done in unsatisfactory conditions. Music was taught mainly in the old green hut in the playground, which became known as 'Mrs Burman's Cottage', with lessons constantly interrupted by balls bouncing against the building. Andrew Cuthbertson, who came to teach piano at the School in 1990, recalled how Mrs Burman, whom

he described as 'a marvellous and very knowledge-able woman', would play an ageing, woodworm-riddled upright Bechstein, keeping an eye on boys singing behind her through a mirror above the piano. The two practice rooms were not sound-proofed. By the end of the 1980s the School calendar featured a series of concerts throughout the year, with performances from the choir and orchestra, smaller music groups and talented soloists. For instance, Prize Giving always featured a short musical programme, the summer concert in the American School was held over two nights and a middle school concert was held in the gym. A jazz band was formed, the house music competition was revived and boys were receiving tuition on a wide range of instruments. Mrs Diack continued to teach piano for some years, remem-bered by Edward Brett as 'a proper musician', with the charm and flair of a continental grande dame. One attraction of her lessons was the blackcurrant fruit pastilles boys were offered. But the number of boys taking Royal School of Music examinations was small and those who did took them at an external examination centre.

Lesley Ralphs was appointed head of art and design in 1982. At interview the Headmaster impressed her as a very warm, kind and welcoming person. A new art room had been opened and Clegg was as keen as she was to make the most of the opportunities it presented. As an exponent of a comprehensive curriculum, he expressed the belief that art was as important for the boys as any other subject. The Headmaster had appointed the right person. 'Art', she said, 'is very exciting because it is limitless.' One boy, Edmund Grouse, remembered how good she was at 'getting us interested through experimentation'. Lesley Ralphs took to her task of reviving a moribund subject with enthusiasm. She boosted the boys' confidence by helping to show them just what they could achieve. Within a couple of years she could write that 'the boys of Arnold

Year 8 leavers' ceramic tiles

House have proved that being "good at Art" is not a gift bestowed on the few'. The quality of their work persuaded the governors to invest in the many display boards that began appearing as art spilled into the rest of the School. The boys loved seeing their work appear on public view. Ceramics was introduced, leading to the tradition of every leaver designing and producing a ceramic tile expressing their own individuality, which became a permanent and growing display. And art was extended across the curriculum, into maths, music and English.

The organisation of the School was gradually overhauled as well. Thompson House appears to have been short-lived but another fourth house was created in 1981, taking the name Brunel after the famous engineer. A middle school was created in between junior and senior schools, all of which had their own teachers in charge. John Prosser, who had been head of two primary schools in Wales, was appointed head of middle school when he joined Arnold House in 1987. An excellent science teacher, he combined this post with the role of deputy head, a position formalised for the first time in 1986, and proved an outstanding success. A kindly and widely liked master, he stood no nonsense. One boy, George Kollakis, remarked in the School magazine in 1994 that 'it's a bad time when you have made Mr Prosser angry. You can tell by the way he moves his moustache.' During the 1990s he was instrumental in developing links between the School and the education department of the Southwest Texas State University in San Marcos, as part of the latter's teacher-training programme. Every year for ten years trainee teachers from the university would spend half a term teaching boys at Arnold House. As John Prosser recalled, 'they brought much to English prep-school life, as they taught the boys a great deal about American and Texan culture'.

In 1990 Philip Pike, himself an outstanding maths teacher, became head of senior school, the responsibilities of which he summed up in 1992:

As Head of the Senior School my responsibilities seem to combine the roles of ombudsman, shop-steward, trouble-shooter and father confessor! I am meant to have the patience of Job and the wisdom of Solomon! I am called upon to listen to endless comments about staff, the meals, too much prep, unfair pink card grades and detentions, and the iniquity of Saturday morning school! But it is not only complaints I hear and in any case I take it as a kind of compliment that the boys feel able to confide in me.

Two years later, he was appointed as a second deputy head while retaining his post in charge of senior school, and retired in 1997.

The junior school Johnny Clegg was happy to leave alone on its own island at No. 3, Loudoun Road. What he did do was appoint a new junior school head in 1980 whom he knew would make the changes the School needed. Chere Hunter took up the post at the age of 30 and left 28 years later. For 18 years her deputy was Nicky Huish, who joined the junior school in 1982. There were still the classes named after the saints, St George, St Andrew, St Nicholas and St Patrick. With their colleagues Marie Kinnear and Janey Roger, Chere Hunter and Nicky Huish maintained the junior school as a home from home for small boys, 'cosy, friendly and warm', as Nicky Huish described it, with small classes, no more than nine or ten strong. Academic lessons took place in the morning, with the afternoons given over to topic-based craftwork. Boys received a sound formal education, which gave them a good grounding in basic literacy and numeracy, as well as in history, geography and religious studies. Every day ended with a story in the hall.

One of the first changes was for the smallest boys to begin attending school all day rather than just half-days, which proved popular with parents. Boys entered at the beginning of the school year

Drama

Following the example set by Diccon Swan, regarded by many boys as an inspirational teacher, drama flourished, growing throughout the School, from the performances put on in the gym by the junior school to senior-school productions staged in the American School with its outstanding facilities. Notable among them were the plays, such as *Drake*, *Billy Liar*, *Peter Pan* and *The Charcoal Burner's Son*, produced by Claire Rankin before she left to take over the Chichester Festival Theatre. *Drake* amazed some boys because of its small, two-sided mobile set, with the queen's throne on one side and a pub on the other. Another notable drama producer was the English teacher, Eileen Barclay. Later productions included *The Sweeney Todd Shock and Roll Show*, *The Mikado* and *Bugsy Malone*.

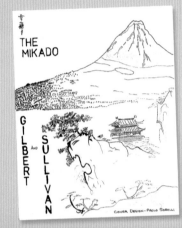

Programmes for *The Mikado* and *Bugsy Malone*

Below: Christian Coulson and Adam Porter in *The Mikado*, 1990

Junior school boys, James Chisnall, David Wolfingdon and Thomas Dehlsen, in the late 1980s

rather than the term in which they turned five. In the Summer term before they started, a taster day was organised for them and their parents. Just as Johnny Clegg was encouraging music and drama in the senior school, so Chere Hunter did the same in the junior school, organising concerts and writing a musical play every Christmas. Claire Rankin also produced Christmas pantomimes and alarmed Nicky Huish one year when she said she would make the boys fly, achieving the illusion by making them appear to float through dry ice. Chere Hunter persuaded the Headmaster to change the uniform, getting rid of the traditional herring-bone overcoats, the very itchy grey woollen jumpers and the dreary taupe mackintoshes.

Parents became more involved, and teaching evenings were organised on reading and basic numeracy and invitations extended to School plays and concerts, in which a Mums' Choir often took part. Trips were arranged to places like Windsor

Castle and frequent visits were made to the local barracks – in the days before security requirements became too onerous, all it took to arrange a visit was a telephone call to the commanding officer. Every summer the boys were taken into the Buckinghamshire countryside, where they could picnic and play in the fields and fresh air, a revelation for those who spent much of their time in apartments with little outside space. There remained a distinct sense of separation between the junior and senior schools. 'It was very much a separate school,' said Chere Hunter. 'We never mixed with the upper school.' There was little mixing between senior-school and junior-school staff – no male staff taught the junior boys – although the younger ones, such as Rhidian Llewellyn, might pop in for coffee first thing in the morning. In the mid-1980s there was brief consideration of acquiring a local nursery school that sent many of its boys on to Arnold House. But the new

classroom block was a higher priority and the governors agreed that the School was unable to afford both.

As part of his belief in widening opportunities for boys, Johnny Clegg introduced a wide range of lunchtime activities on Mondays and Fridays. By the early 1980s boys could choose from cooking, bridge, chess, the geography and science clubs and two small groups learning Russian and Italian. In its early days there was a certain element of anarchy in the science club. Edward Brett recalled spending his time mass-producing explosive concoctions as the boys were allowed to play with the chemicals in the laboratory. On one occasion he had just made a mortar-full when another boy, heating a fork over a Bunsen flame, found it too hot to handle and dropped it in the mortar. The vessel and its contents

exploded, blowing a hole in the ceiling, and leading unsurprisingly to Brett's suspension.

This, of course, was not the only mischief the boys got up to. The sweet shop at St John's Wood tube station was a magnet during break for some boys, who would bound over the wall behind the playground and nip into the shop before returning without being spotted by staff. Another boy would hang out of the classroom window and another was reprimanded for catching a lift on the back of a milk-float coming back from an event at UCS. One boy, mooning at his classroom window, failed to take into account that it overlooked the front playground, from where a party of passing parents had an excellent view.

The boys also engaged in their own unofficial pastimes. A popular craze during the early 1980s

Chess has always been popular and in the 1980s it was introduced as a lunchtime activity. Peyto Burnett (left) and Jonathan Edgelow (right) pondering the next move

Activities programme

The activities programme grew steadily during the 1980s. Competition was encouraged between the houses in all sorts of subjects from general knowledge and current affairs to verse speaking, Shakespearian recitation and French. Debating was introduced by John Prosser. In 1990, for instance, the boys debated Halloween with girls from South Hampstead Junior High School. As part of this, parties of boys were taken regularly to the Houses of Parliament. By the time activities were consolidated into one longer midweek session in 1993, boys could study opera, the history of medicine and modern technology, Egyptology, ornithology, wine appreciation and cookery, learn calligraphy or help catalogue and process new library books, play chess and other board games, jog, juggle or maintain bicycles. Jonathan Naggar, who left the School in 1982, had never found his Headmaster approachable until he began learning to play bridge with him – 'this was the one time I saw him in a warmer situation'. Ed Sanders, who joined the School in 1980, remembered playing a unique version of

Year 3 visit to Whitehall to see the State Opening of Parliament, 1985

Scrabble. Devised by Miss O'Donnell, it used Cyrillic letters for English words as a way of encouraging the boys to learn the Cyrillic alphabet. All this, felt Ed, was part of the School's purpose in sending boys out of Arnold House as well-rounded individuals.

was what Edward Brett described as 'the scratch-and-sniff sticker racket'. Jonathan Naggar confessed that he made a lot of money from trading stickers. It was a market he fuelled by investing all his money in a wide selection of stickers he brought back from his holidays in the USA. He made a great return, something approved of by his entrepreneurial father, but rather less so by Johnny Clegg, who summoned young Jonathan to his study and instructed him to scale down his trading. When James Hyman recorded in his schoolboy diary during 1982 that 'Sniffy Gang stickers are in England!', presumably the bottom fell out of the market.

More ambitious excursions were organised. To help with this, the School acquired its first minibus in 1984. As well as visits to the usual London destinations, such as the Zoo, the Tower and the Museum of London, more distant trips were arranged. In 1983 the senior boys were taken after Common Entrance to Paris for a long weekend. In 1990 when one form visited York for the day, the boys took in Jorvik Viking history centre – 'we came', wrote Charles Chown, 'to a part where you saw a man sitting on the loo' – and the National Railway Museum. 'I liked the trains,' wrote Adam Lorenz. 'There were buttons you pressed, and things like trains moved; there were lights too and chimney sweeps and windmills.' Overseas visits became common. As well as trips to France, a group travelled to West Germany in 1984 to play football, and parties of boys went skiing in Italy, Austria and Yugoslavia. Edward Brett remembered a visit to Greece with Mr Stobbs and Miss O'Donnell, with

First XI football team, left, and cricket team, below, 1976

boys taking sips of Mr Stobbs's ouzo during their stay in Athens.

Lighter entertainment was introduced. There was a School disco held in the gym, which, recollected David Burr, usually turned out to be 'just the boys running around in the playground and trying to avoid the girls'. At end-of-term parties boys could bring their favourite snacks. The tables were prepared before break but no boy was permitted to start eating until break had ended.

None of this was intended to diminish the importance of sport. Johnny Clegg was himself a keen sportsman. Again Clegg's aim was to expand the opportunities available alongside the traditional sports of football, cricket, swimming and boxing. He appointed a head of PE, John Brierley, a talented Scottish triple-jumper. He retained the tradition of devoting every Tuesday and Thursday afternoon to games. Inter-house sporting competitions were

Cricket at Canons Park, late 1980s

organised. Squash was offered at courts in Hampstead, hockey was revived on the lower playground, tennis was played at Canons Park, basketball, judo and fencing were started. Hockey, remembered Jonathan Naggar, was a fast and furious game on the hard surface of the School playground, and the slower surface of a grass pitch at his senior school would come as a disappointment to him.

Rugby was re-introduced and the School achieved its first win in the revived sport by 12 points to ten against Douai in 1982. Within a few years an Arnold House team was entering the National Schoolboy Sevens at Rosslyn Park. Cross-country was conducted around the bridleway on the Hampstead Heath Extension. Boys competed in their first cross-country championship, after which reluctant runners were compelled to endure cleansing showers despite all their protestations.

Johnny Clegg, who had been amazed on coming to the School to discover that few boys ever showered after matches, insisted that they did. In the second week following this edict, quite a number of boys, embarrassed at appearing naked in the showers, came equipped with swimming trunks. For Ed Sanders, David Burr and Daniel Hahn, who were all at the School in the 1980s, travelling to Canons Park for the first time filled them with dread because of the prospect of communal showers. A new properly equipped gym was an instant success, making it, as recorded the School magazine in July 1981, 'a paradise for running, jumping, rolling, tumbling, climbing and boxing'. What the magazine did not reveal was the feat of young Charles Falk, who climbed on top of the building's roof, declaring as loudly as possible, 'I am the king!'

Instead of being confined to the annual Sports Day, athletics was coached throughout the season, using the track at Parliament Hill. New events, including the shot put and discus, were added, and in 1983 boys took part for the first time in the London Area Prep Schools Athletics Meeting at the West London Stadium. A separate Sports Day was initiated for the junior school. Clegg began the practice of taking boys down to nearby Lord's for cricket nets. Boxing continued for several years, and it remained a daunting experience for many young boys. Edward Brett recalled that although the boys began using the softer modern boxing gloves, they also had the much harder old-fashioned gloves which could really hurt. Brett's friend Jonathan Naggar, on the other hand, loved boxing.

Clegg never liked boxing for young boys. He hated watching boys crumple up in tears. At one tournament bout between two friends, when one hit the other, and both of them began to cry, Clegg insisted on taking over the bell, ringing it as soon as a blow was landed by either boy. He was always determined to bring an end to boxing despite some opposition from the governors. The board eventually agreed to phase out the sport and it ceased at the end of the Summer term in 1988. By then School hockey matches were being played by 'A' and 'B' teams and an inter-school swimming gala had been organised at UCS. One criticism of sport from boys at the School in the late 1970s and early 1980s was that it remained too exclusive and there was too much pressure to perform at an early age. This began to change from 1989, following the appointment of Rick Martin as head of PE and games, who expanded the number of School teams to enable more boys to represent the School. In 1990 Martin, with John Faulkner, who was a talented sportsman as well as an excellent teacher, inaugurated what became the traditional autumn half-term rugby tour of the Lake District. Cricket tours were later added. Arnold House also hosted a seven-a-side football tournament.

There were some outstanding individual performances. The cricket First XI enjoyed a golden year in 1983. The team was placed joint first in the Colet Court Cricket Festival. Mark Lowrey scored more than 600 runs, including one century and a score of 98 not out. The captain, Robert Nelson, took most of the wickets, including two hat-tricks. By the end of the decade the Arnold House gymnastic team, as regional prep-school champions, had won the bronze medal at the National Gymnastics Team Championships. In 1993 Alex Braithwaite and Alex Shields won bronze medals in the National Prep Schools Judo Championships and were invited together with Alex Kollakis to take part in an international team match in Holland.

One of the pranks boys repeated week in, week out, was to dare each other to infiltrate the pavilion at Canons Park and raid the tea laid out for the School teams. The raids, recalled Charles Falk, were planned with military precision and usually succeeded. On one occasion there appeared to be just a single piece of cake left out on the table. Sneaking in, the boys snatched a bit of it, scarpering as they heard the sound of approaching footsteps. They took refuge in the changing room, only to be confronted by Johnny Clegg, holding what was left of the cake. Tea had been cleared away with the exception of the cake left especially for the Headmaster. 'Falk! Was this you?' he demanded, rubbing the crumbling cake into the boy's face.

The lack of permanent playing fields constantly exercised the board of governors. 'It has always', noted the governors' minutes in February 1987, 'been one of the Board's aims to purchase playing fields.' It was noted that an opportunity had arisen to do just that. It turned out that the owners of the playing fields at Canons Park, long used by the School, were selling them off. The Working Men's College was – and still is – the oldest surviving adult education institute in Europe, having been founded in 1854. Associated with the Cooperative

Above: Front cover of the Canons Park Appeal brochure

Above right: A drawing from the School magazine, 1993

Movement and the Christian Socialists, it was born of the same tradition that later led to the Worker's Educational Association. The College at the time was short of cash and was seeking to raise urgently needed funds from the sale. It proved to be quite a saga that was drawn out over several years. The College sold the whole seven-acre site to a developer, McAlpine, before planning consent had been granted. This aroused considerable, well-organised local opposition. Alan Lipscomb, by then chairman of governors, persuaded his colleagues that rather than wringing their hands, it was in their interests to join forces with the scheme's opponents. The campaign against the plans influenced their rejection by the local planning authority. This handed the advantage to the School. Lipscomb, accompanied by his predecessor as chairman, Richard Roney, an experienced lawyer, approached McAlpine with an offer to buy the land. Thanks to Roney, the negotiations were ultimately concluded with success on 23 December 1991. Alan Lipscomb always regarded this as his prime achievement during his time as a governor.

He told the board in June 1992 that 'the Canons Park Project had been a watershed'.

Johnny Clegg summed up the importance of securing Canons Park in his report for 1992:

> Just what that means to Arnold House came across to me very strongly indeed when we played the Dragon School on May 30th as the first, home, Saturday fixture on our own ground. To see the Tennis Club occupying the Courts, the Bowling Club having an exciting match, the West Indian Cricket Club attached to Canons Park having the most extraordinary Caribbean match in the far corner whilst we ourselves enjoyed a thoroughly good and entertaining match with the Dragon School, made us feel very proud.

The development of plans for the repair, refurbishment and improvement of facilities at Canons Park led to the deeper involvement of individual governors. Legal requirements resulted in the formation of a separate company to manage the playing fields. The five-year rolling redevelopment programme would drain the School's reserves and

made it imperative not only that every effort should be made to recruit external users for the grounds but also that an appeal was made for funds.

The acquisition of Canons Park had been preceded by other physical improvements at Loudoun Road. On 10 February 1981 the Duchess of Gloucester opened a new block situated between No. 1 and No. 3 which included more classrooms as well as the new art and craft room and the new gym. Plans were then made to replace the temporary building on the playground with another extension comprising a new science laboratory. Music would move to the old laboratory and new changing facilities with showers would be built on top of the gym, with further classrooms above. It was this building that allowed the old lab to be converted into a music room and the small cramped classrooms at the top of No. 1, Loudoun Road, to be vacated. It was funded partly by increasing numbers for the first time since the 1950s, with the roll expanding to 225, partly from existing reserves and partly from an appeal. The governors also had to take into consideration the School's position as a leaseholder. Every new building brought with it an increase in the rent paid to the Eyre Estate. The new building

THIS BUILDING
GENEROUSLY DONATED BY PAST & PRESENT PARENTS,
OLD BOYS AND FRIENDS OF ARNOLD HOUSE SCHOOL
WAS OPENED BY
H.R.H. THE DUCHESS OF GLOUCESTER
ON 10 TH. FEBRUARY 1981

was finally completed in 1988, when it was opened by Sir Godfrey Le Quesne, the distinguished lawyer, also a parent and chairman of the appeal committee.

The aims of the Headmaster, backed by the governors, in expanding curricular and extra-curricular opportunities and improving physical facilities enjoyed the support of School staff who played a crucial role in making many of these improvements possible. While Johnny Clegg told the governors in 1983 that newly appointed staff had helped to improve the atmosphere within the School, the welcoming environment found by many newcomers owed much to those already there. For George Lester, who joined Arnold House in 1982 after teaching in Kenya, it was this environment throughout the School that meant

The Duchess of Gloucester opens the new building, 1981

The new building in 1981

he was still teaching there 30 years later. He found his colleagues often colourful but always welcoming, accepting and tolerant. Lesley Ralphs found she was overwhelmed with offers of help from staff when she joined the School. Andrew Cuthbertson recalled that when he was appointed in 1990, 'The very first day I felt very happy here. There was just something about the place. My colleagues were so welcoming and I just felt at home straightaway.' Still teaching in 2013, he reflected he had never had any wish to move on; 'that feeling I had on the first day has stayed with me all the way through'.

Several long-serving staff would retire during this period, including John Robson and Elizabeth Diack. Others included Roddy Williams, the senior master and head of maths, who spent 20 years at the School until his retirement in 1990. An able teacher and a compassionate man, his eyesight was very poor, and the boys respected the way in which he overcame this disability. Ken Stobbs served 12 years as head of geography, also retiring in 1990. A

colourful character with a pronounced Scottish accent, he taught by circulating purple cyclostyled notes on which he would base classroom games to test and instil knowledge. The notes came with the heady perfume of the copying ink which the boys took delight in sniffing. As one of them, David Burr, later said, 'you would inhale the knowledge'. One of Ken Stobbs' frequent refrains was 'Learn your notes, boy!' and several of the topics he taught are still fixed in the minds of many boys from that era, such as 'Cocoa in Ghana' and 'Rice in India'. In 1993 Gill Stern retired after 14 years on the staff.

Some who made their mark stayed only briefly. Among this latter group were people like Claire Rankin, Rhidian Llewellyn and Duncan Bruce-Lockhart. Llewellyn taught English and history and would later become head of Papplewick School. He would tell the story of his idiosyncratic interview by Johnny Clegg. The Headmaster's first question was, 'Do you like cricket?', and on receiving a positive answer, suggested the two of them went into the playground, saying 'I will bat and you bowl.' Many other applicants experienced this laid-back approach to interviewing, which more often than not involved a cosy chat in a comfy chair over a glass of sherry. Duncan Bruce-Lockhart was a larger-than-life character, a talented rugby player, popular with all the boys. When he left in 1989, his form emptied their pockets and collected nearly a hundred pounds for him; many boys were in tears.

Some staff made their mark and stayed. George Lester came as a fourth-form teacher, reflecting in 1992 that his role required 'a good deal of humour, patience and tolerance. For much of the time it's an uphill battle trying to get boys at this stage to become more accountable for their own work, books, prep, kit etc, and there are still one or two who still, after several terms, arrive late, bookless, prepless and sockless.' His colleague Chere Hunter later observed of him that

> George was always the life and soul of every party we had – and there were many in those days, both at School and at Johnny and Gilly's house in Hampstead. He was warm, witty and rather naughty but a great conversationalist and also a good listener who kept everyone amused until the wine had been flowing for too long and then he would go very quiet indeed!

Johnny Clegg had high expectations of every member of staff he appointed but he also welcomed the new ideas that younger teachers brought with them, as he made clear in the letters of appointment he sent to newcomers. He also appreciated the effort staff made on behalf of the School and those who had stayed to work late he would often send home with bottles of wine. Nicky Huish described him as a wise man, with whom a conversation could sometimes be disconcerting as the Headmaster paused before he found the answer he wished to give.

The expansion of the School, in terms of boys, activities and facilities, made its management more complex. For many years it had been sufficient to leave administration in the hands of the Headmaster while finances were handled at a distance by a firm of City accountants, with a designated governor acting as Governor Treasurer. As the daily management of the School's finances became more complicated and consuming, it became clear this was a task that could no longer be left to the head or his secretary. This was compounded by Johnny Clegg's acknowledgement that administration was his weak spot. He relied heavily on his secretary although initially several of them were unable to keep up with the long hours he worked, which spilled over into the school holidays. Gilly Clegg acted as a stop-gap before the appointment firstly of Terry Strong and then Rachel Gostage. As one friend later wrote, he was 'interested in people, not paperwork'. He had so little idea about the latter, said Penny Williams, who became his assistant secretary in 1989, that he had been replying at length even to sales circulars that came through the post. The tapes he dictated at home over the weekend came back complete with a soundtrack of children shouting, dogs barking and glasses clinking.

John Allain,
bursar 1989–97

Teaching staff, 1992. Back row, left to right: Keith Mallinson, Teresa Burman, Gill Stern, George Lester, Peter Ward, Ben Broch, Kevin Maynard, Alistair Newman, John Grey, John Faulkner, Andrew Cuthbertson.
Front row, left to right: Eirlys Sayle, Rick Martin, Katherine Benham-Crosswell, Lesley Ralphs, John Prosser, Nicky Huish, William Murphy, Sarah Rosenthal, Chere Hunter, Philip Pike, Lucilla Garner

In 1983 the governors finally agreed to appoint the School's first bursar, Captain Denis Roe. His duties were soon expanded when Johnny Clegg made too many offers to too many boys, confessing to the governors that 'he simply had not appreciated that so many places had been promised and that he was entirely to blame'. The responsibility for regulating the number of admissions became part of the bursar's brief. Captain Roe served six years before being succeeded in 1989 by former Metropolitan Police commander John Allain. Allain, a modest and unassuming man with a great sense of humour and a penchant for red braces, made an excellent foil for Johnny Clegg. He recorded in his diary that the Headmaster had very quickly delegated to him the unpleasant task of making sure the boys ate their semolina at lunchtime. Allain was a talented chess player and encouraged the

game among the boys, running School chess even beyond his retirement in 1997. Further complications arose with the acquisition of Canons Park and an accountant was recruited to support the bursar in 1992. With the growing demand for places and the admission of more boys, recruitment and registration became much more taxing. Penny Williams would later concentrate on this area as registrar alongside the head and the bursar.

The governors played a key role. Richard Roney, who himself had taken over from Colin Winser as chairman, was succeeded by Alan Lipscomb in 1984. There had been some tension between the board and the Headmaster, which was unsurprising as the former tended to dislike the changes proposed by the latter. With his commercial experience, Lipscomb helped to bring a much more businesslike and formal approach to the board.

Governors received more and better quality information and they came to know each other better, partly through the annual dinners organised by Lipscomb and his wife Pat, which helped develop greater unity on the board. It was only in the early 1990s that the near monopoly of former pupils on the governing body was broken when Lipscomb invited a former parent, Colin St Johnston, to join, rather to the discontent of one or two older members.

The governors had made the right appointment in 1977. Johnny Clegg was a huge influence on the development of Arnold House. A warm and charismatic man, he charmed everyone he met, working his personal magic with boys, staff and parents, and developing an extensive network of contacts throughout the public-school world. It was his desire to remain in touch with the boys that led him to persist on teaching a full timetable, even though it was frequently interrupted by other demands on his time. Whatever the merits of the bonus-malus system Clegg introduced to the School, it illustrated how much time he could spend with the boys. The system rewarded boys with bonuses and punished them with maluses. Every week each boy would present his exercise book to the Headmaster, who would sign each one, total up the marks and distribute as a reward the required number of sweets from a huge jar in his study. On a boy's birthday, Clegg would reach into his pocket and bring out as a gift what he called 'a little silver', usually a ten-pence piece.

It was through contact with the boys that he felt he could influence them. At the table he headed at lunchtimes, for instance, he expected boys to ask only for small or medium helpings if they wanted seconds, since asking for a large helping was taken as a sign of greed, and the head would rap the knuckles of the offender with a spoon. He expected them to assume responsibility. In 1989 he introduced a system which recognised attitude and

performance through the award of ties for specific categories (Games, Attitude and Example in the Classroom, Service to the Community and Awareness of Responsibility towards Oneself and towards the Rest of the School) decided by a common-room vote. At parents' evenings it was obvious, according to one of them, that 'he knew his boys very well'.

He was no soft touch, either with parents or boys. As Gilly Clegg remembered, when a steely glint appeared in his blue eyes, people knew not to push him any further. He made clear to parents when they had outstayed their welcome at parents' evening by getting out the vacuum cleaner to hasten their departure and allow his staff to get

Outside No. 1, Loudoun Road, mid-1980s.
Top row, left to right: John Bradbury, Ashley Usiskin, Andreas Lemos.
Front row, left to right: Mark Sorrel, Simon McCoombe

home. For some boys, their overriding impression was of an imposing Headmaster, someone who, in Jonathan Naggar's words, was 'a little bit of a scary man'. James Hyman, Naggar's contemporary, agreed, but could also see the head's great sense of humour, and his affection for his pupils. Teresa Burman would describe how the head's sternness masked a natural compassion. She told of how two nine-year-olds were sent to him for fighting out of bounds, turning up covered in mud from head to toe. Restraining his natural inclination to laugh, Clegg led them straight to the bathroom, ran a bath and told them to clean off every last trace of mud. Clean uniforms were obtained and very soon a pair of freshly scrubbed boys was back in class. 'Mr Clegg was later seen on his knees,' she wrote, 'shirt sleeves rolled, trying to erase the very black ring from around the bath.'

While Clegg exercised discipline when it was necessary, more usually he deployed every ounce of his extensive charm to win others over. He had, said one parent, Alan Warner, 'a lovely light touch with parents ... a lovely light touch with the boys ... people naturally warmed to him'. As Charles Falk admitted, 'I adored him'. This was quite a common reaction among the boys. Ed Sanders believed that 'everyone loved him – he was what made Arnold House for our generation'. Clegg engendered the same degree of loyalty and affection previous generations had given to George Smart. Looking back on his days at Arnold House, Paul Kassabian, one of Clegg's head boys, remarked, 'I truly see it as the foundation stone for my education. Somehow, even though it wasn't the first school I went to, I see the path of my life as starting there, and I couldn't have wished for a better beginning.' Clegg took over George Smart's mantle in maintaining links with many boys after they left Arnold House. One boy so hated his boarding school that, running away, and making a call from a telephone box, he insisted he would not speak with anyone

other than Mr Clegg, who set out to bring him back and spent hours talking to the boy about his anxieties. Once boys were old enough to attend the annual '42 Club dinner, the Headmaster would insist on buying a drink for each of 'the Clegg boys'.

Gilly Clegg was as much a part of the School as her husband. Staff, parents and boys enjoyed on countless occasions the hospitality of Johnny and Gilly at their home in Briardale Gardens. Not only did she act as Johnny's secretary, for a time she also took over the role of housekeeper following an accident to the previous incumbent who had professed to be 50 but whose doctor informed the School that she was actually 20 years older and would not be returning to work. For the boys, Gilly was a very visible presence, whether running cookery classes or just helping them with their problems.

Clegg summed up his philosophy in the School magazine in July 1981, writing that 'my own priority is that every single boy in the School should be happy'. He described the importance for him of what were always loosely alluded to as the five 'C's. 'I talk to all the children about the five concepts of Kindness, Courtesy, Compassion, Care and Concern ... the actual passing of the Common Entrance, or the gaining of a Scholarship, should never be considered the be all and end all of a boy's life at Preparatory School, but should be but a part of the many aspects of what we strive to do for the children.' Parents understood this approach, even as some of them engaged private tuition for their sons, appreciating that at Arnold House academic achievement never overrode the emotional well-being of the boys or the development of their individual talents. Jon and Carlyn Zehner sent four boys to the School. They wanted to find a school that shared a similar ethos to the one from which they had brought their boys in New York. As soon as they entered Arnold House, recalled Carlyn, 'We knew this was it'. It was warm and homely, just like Johnny Clegg, who always seemed to be 'followed by

Drawings by Damian Crook and Jonathan Hazan from the School magazine, 1986

Prefects, 1981.
From left to right:
Top row: Phillip
Ruhemann and Neil
Aitken. Bottom row:
Richard Finston,
Robert Harley,
Robert Dowler,
John Crossick and
Jonathan Levy

a little cloud of happiness'. Jon Zehner summed up the ethos of the School in two words, 'community and humanity'. Carlyn Zehner added that, 'The whole warmth and sense of community we felt as parents the boys also felt'. It was a school, recalled one pupil, Edmund Grouse, where boys could retain their individuality, for the pack mentality never really existed at Arnold House. 'You were allowed to be who you wanted to be and no one compelled you to be otherwise.' As a small school, with small year groups, Arnold House was a tight-knit and collegiate place, with a strong sense of camaraderie, where year groups happily intermingled. It was a place, said John Prosser, 'where boys had a sense of fun and a sense of achievement'.

Courtesy, recalled Rick Martin, was a constant characteristic of the School from the polite welcome he received on his very first morning from a red-blazered young boy who had unwittingly turned up on the day before term began. At the end of his very first lesson in School John Prosser was amazed to have a pupil say thank you. This ethos certainly had an impact on a number of boys as they reflected on

their time at Arnold House. Henry Bevan, who left in 1994, recalled how 'manners, politeness, trustworthiness, civility and thought for others seemed to form just as much a part of the curriculum as maths or English'. James Kilner, who left in 1992, remarked that the School was 'such a friendly, polite place that its indelible mark is probably fairness and perspective'; while his brother Charlie, who left in 1995, believed that Arnold House had 'made me into a polite and well-mannered boy'.

Compassion, care and concern might expect to be expressed through a school's pastoral care system. Although this was never overt at Arnold House, it was very evident. Edmund Grouse remembered his junior school form teacher, Mrs Rosenthal, 'this wonderful orb, this incredibly kind and incredibly lovely woman, very strict but very kind'. When Edmund felt he was being bullied by a couple of boys, one of whom remains his friend to this day, he looked to Mrs Rosenthal. She quietly explained why his antagonists might have turned to bullying, spoke to each of them individually and then all together, and a line was drawn under the matter. For Grouse, this exemplified how staff 'engaged with you, even at that tiny age'. Edward Brett reflected that

> This was a very happy school. The boys had a great experience growing up at the School and School performance and results were strong including many well-deserved scholarships. Individual staff were very compassionate and got on very well with the boys. The School had compassion, tolerance and a strong academic ethos, but most importantly a lovely group of boys that got on.

It was a happy experience for many boys. James Hyman left the School in 1982. 'I genuinely had such a lovely time. I never felt under any pressure. I never noticed any bullying at the School. I can't recall anything bad about the School. All my memories are good.' The diary he kept shows how for small boys little events loomed large, revealing, he says, 'these tiny little moments that mattered so much'. March 1980 was typical – on 6 March 'we had lots of adventures on the tube coming back from boxing'; on 10 March he recorded that lunch had consisted of chicken and the hated rice pudding; on 11 March it was noteworthy that Mr Williams had chalk on his trousers. Arnold House was a happy place for young boys and a recurring theme among many reminiscences is the lifelong friendships formed by many boys at such a young age.

A drawing from the School magazine, 1992

'Conquer We Shall'
1994–2005

6

As education changed, Johnny Clegg found it hard to adapt. Managing a school was becoming ever more complex. Requirements to ensure every school had the relevant policies and procedures in place to protect and support staff and pupils were becoming more onerous. Clegg hated having less time to get to know the boys, but he loved his work. He had already won a two-year extension of his contract from the governors. But when the letter arrived from the board reminding him that he was expected to retire at the age of 60 in 1990, as specified in his contract, it came as a shock. He had either failed to read his contract properly or forgotten all about it. Although the governors could see that the Headmaster was being overtaken by the times, he did not feel ready for retirement. The news alarmed parents. A petition was organised. A meeting was held between representatives of the governors and representatives of the parents. The compromise allowed the Headmaster to remain in post until he was 64. It was not an easy

time either for the governors or for the Headmaster. For a while Johnny Clegg suffered from ill health and John Prosser ably ran the School in his stead.

None of this should detract from what Johnny Clegg achieved for Arnold House. One need only read the new School prospectus prepared during his last year to appreciate how much the School had changed since his appointment in 1977. The School now comprised three linked buildings with ample space for play, and included a gym, art and craft studio, computer studies room and up-to-date science laboratory. The School owned its own playing fields at Canons Park, which provided pitches for cricket, football and hockey, tennis courts, a large pavilion and changing rooms. Boys

Above: Sports Day, Canons Park, 2002

Left: Chess team, 2000

had the opportunity to take up football, rugby, hockey and cricket, swimming, athletics and tennis, cross-country running, table tennis and badminton, judo, fencing and basketball. Annual tours were arranged for the cricket, rugby and football teams. Other organised activities, now moved to Wednesday afternoons, ranged from bridge, chess, computing and cooking to debating, juggling and drama. Art, including pottery, music and computer studies were all part of the curriculum, and Greek had been reintroduced for the abler boys. There were two choirs, an orchestra and a jazz band, and an art exhibition was held every year.

Jazz band, 1996–7, with staff David Clewlow, Rick Martin and Kate Davies

The consequences of all this were outlined in two tributes to the retiring Headmaster, one from his chairman of governors, Alan Lipscomb, the other from a parent, Elaine Moylan. Lipscomb wrote of

an explosion in the number of activities a boy can pursue. This variety of interests teaches boys to be flexible and adaptable; it tests their response and enthusiasm for new things. It also seeks out hidden talent and gives the chance for a boy to develop and grow in self-reliance and esteem. It encourages the beginnings of self-education.

Clegg achieved a happy family atmosphere based on care and consideration for others. Elaine Moylan wrote how Clegg 'knows [the boys] and cares about them. His concern goes beyond getting a boy out of trouble once he's got into it. He feels responsible for making sure that the boys leave the School as decent human beings, with a strong sense of goodness and fair play ... for me the essence of Mr Clegg is his humanity.' He departed held in high regard by boys, parents and staff, his farewell article in the School magazine giving his thanks 'to all the parents, the staff and to the boys for making Gilly's and my life at Arnold House such a truly happy and richly satisfying one'.

His successor, just the fifth person to head the School in nine decades, was Nicholas Allen. Aged 41, Allen was married with three children; his two sons, Hugh and Ralph, entered the School. Following prep school, Allen attended Bedales and then studied history and archaeology at Exeter university. After taking his teaching qualification, he taught at prep schools in Cheshire, Sussex, Hertfordshire and Suffolk. Prior to his appointment as head of Arnold House, he had spent seven years as headmaster of Ipswich Prep School, the long-established junior department of Ipswich School. Sharp, focused and driven, he was, in contrast to Johnny Clegg, a shy and self-effacing

Nicholas Allen with Senior boys

man which made him seem more distant to those who had known his predecessor, while his formality tended to hide his kindness and dry sense of humour.

Taking over from a long-serving, successful and highly regarded headmaster would have been a difficult task for any successor. Nicholas Allen appreciated the School's strengths. He wrote in a School newsletter at the beginning of his first term in September 1994 that, 'I knew from the moment I first had dealings with Arnold House that it was the school for me! The happy and purposeful atmosphere, the dedicated staff and the unaffected assurance of the boys I met when I was in London at interview made the prospect of this headship a most attractive one. I have not been disappointed and I have grown to realise day by day how much I owe my predecessor.' But he also recognised, as had the governors, that change was needed. Unlike Johnny Clegg, Nicholas Allen's strengths lay in administration and management. Once again the

Nicholas Allen awarding Freddie Fox his cup at Prize Giving, St John's Wood Synagogue, early 2000s

governors had appointed the right person for the right time. The need for change had become apparent to him even before he had taken up his post, with people queuing up to tell him either that nothing needed to be changed or that everything had to be changed at once. In particular reform was required in those areas of administration where Johnny Clegg had always confessed he was weak. The evolution of School management from a peripheral to a central part of headship and the development of a much more professional approach was already well underway at many other schools. A few years later Allen summed up his role for the School magazine:

What do I do all day as a 'modern' headmaster? Write, read, appraise, interview, appoint, devise policies, delegate whenever possible, report, chair meetings, lead training, deliver the curriculum, raise funds, prepare for inspection, monitor, listen, 'walk the talk' or whatever the latest

management buzz-phrase is ... But for bits of most days I get back to the refreshing basics: have lunch with the boys, take assembly and hymn practice, stand on duty at the gate in the morning and do a bit of teaching.

It was time for Arnold House to catch up. As Nicholas Allen reflected, 'A lot of things were pretty old-fashioned'. It needed effective systems, clear structures and greater transparency. Allen found that resistance to change, which had tasked his predecessor, was still in evidence. He decided to change the date for Prize Giving. Traditionally held in December, it required a number of prize winners who had left the previous term to return to take up their awards, which was not always possible. Taking advice from staff, Allen decided that in future it would be held in the Summer term. It was soon conveyed to him that George Smart was very unhappy about the move. Allen stood firm; it was a decision for him to take as Headmaster.

George Smart and
Nicholas Allen at a
'42 Club dinner, late
1990s

It was around this time that George Smart attended his last governors' meeting, as subsequent illness prevented him from coming to further meetings. He had had the satisfaction some years earlier of unveiling his own portrait at the School. It was commissioned by the governors in 1988 from Diccon Swan, the former English teacher turned successful portrait painter, and hangs on the wall above the stairs in No. 1, Loudoun Road. The consensus among the boys at the time was that, in the words of Tobias Astor, Smart's portrait 'made him look quite a lot younger'. Smart himself regarded it as an honour he ill deserved. Increasingly deaf, he resigned from the governors in February 1995, when he assumed the office of Life President. He died at the age of 95 on 8 July 2000. It had been 63 years since he had secured the future of Arnold House by purchasing the School from Miss Hanson. He had steered the School safely through the war years. Above all, he had laid down the values intrinsically associated with the School, which had played a major part in establishing its successful post-war reputation. A memorial service held in St John's Wood Church in October 2000 was attended by more than 150 people.

Nicholas Allen was not a man who pursued change for its own sake. The first development plan drawn up for the School in 1994 was guided by two key principles, to hold on to what was good and to do what was best for the boys. He perceived the aim of the School to be the education of boys to become 'really moral beings'. His philosophy had much in common with that of his predecessors. In 2000 he wrote in the School magazine that

> Arnold House has always striven to provide and strengthen the values young boys will need in life: courtesy, kindness, tolerance and a desire to explore the possibilities which the world has to offer. The range of opportunities open to boys today is greater than it was nearly a century ago. I hope that boys today will learn the value of gaining skills and knowledge which will sustain them in later life.

He believed that the School should be a place where boys and staff were happy to belong. He sought to encapsulate the School's ethos in a written code of conduct, something that had never been done before. It set out in practical terms how every member of the School community could express those virtues – courtesy, consideration, honesty, tolerance and kindness – for so long a part of the upbringing of every boy at Arnold House. It summed up the School's approach by suggesting that, 'if there were only one principle delineated in the Code of Conduct, it would be "Do as you would be done to"'. Several years later, in 2004, Allen was able to reflect of the School that 'on balance, affection, care, consideration for others and respect tend to win out over hostility, rivalry, indifference and inconsiderate rudeness'. In the same issue of the School magazine one young boy, Freddie Villiers, recorded the most striking memory of his first year – 'I remember when a big boy was kind to me when I fell over in the playground on my first day.' The School still uses the same code today.

Jane Darcy, Head of English, teaching in the late 1990s

Penny Williams, registrar since 1999

Over time a whole series of changes were made. Out went the requirement that a boy's age determined which form he entered, which had created an imbalance in numbers among the forms. For the first time boys were assessed prior to admission. With a constant demand for places, the registration system and the organisation of visits for prospective parents became more and more complex. This led to the appointment of Penny Williams as registrar in 1999, who helped to create a much more orderly and transparent approach. In 2004 senior boys first conducted prospective parents on tours around the School, without any guidance as to what they should say – it proved to be a great success. More emphasis was placed on ability and achievement in organising senior forms. To give more boys more responsi-

bility, weekly duty teams were introduced. Pastoral care was placed in the hands of form teachers, form periods were extended as a result, and a structured programme of Personal, Health and Social Education was introduced.

This led to the creation of the lower school, alongside the upper and middle schools, covering boys in Years 3–4, where they began to learn to become more independent and self-reliant. This was further refined in 2005 when the School was split in two, with the lower school (which very soon reverted to the title of junior school) covering boys in their first four years (the first two being classified as the pre-prep section), and the senior school taking boys for the second half of their time. Both halves of the School, junior and senior, became integrated for the first time through the

The statue of St Michael

Sir William Reid Dick

The statue of St Michael was presented to the School in the 1920s. It was sculpted by William Reid Dick, RA, whose son was at Arnold House at the time. The statue is made of plaster and is the maquette for the stone version commissioned to stand in the Kitchener Memorial Chapel in St Paul's Cathedral, where it can be found today.

For many years, the plaster statue stood on the south wall of Arnold House where years of frost and rain took their toll, despite frequent coats of Snowcem. In 1999, the statue was taken down and restored. It was placed high on the wall by the glass doors in the link block in March 2001. This may not be St Michael's final resting place, but one thing is for sure, the statue will never again stand outside, exposed to the elements.

Right: Andrew
Mason and friends
recreating the
famous Beatles
album cover near
the school, 2002

creation of one common room for all members of staff. Both parts of the School held their athletics sports on the same day, one in the morning, one in the afternoon, rather than separately. All the forms were renamed and the educational developments, such as records of achievement, that had passed the School by were adopted, with all the paperwork that necessarily entailed. IT became integrated across the curriculum. The bonus-malus system was abolished and greater emphasis was placed on rewarding boys. The uniform was revised, initially allowing seniors to wear long trousers for most of the year and later extending this opportunity to most boys, and dispensing with grey shirts in favour of green polo shirts and red fleeces worn alongside the traditional blazers. The School adopted its own pay scale, maintaining the differential over the maintained sector. Interviews became more professional, uniform staff contracts were introduced and staff appraisals brought in.

In his initial assessment of the School for the governors in the autumn of 1994 Allen had indicated that there was too little space for the younger boys, who made up two-thirds of the School's entry. He also suggested better music and library facilities were needed. The additional impetus for change, as it had been several times in the past, was an inspection of the School. The team from the Independent Schools Joint Council (ISJC), as it was then, visited the School in 1996. They were impressed by the quality of work, variety of teaching methods, standard of pastoral care and the opportunities for development inside and outside the classroom. They were particularly struck by the relaxed and natural good manners and kind and tolerant attitude of the boys. But they highlighted the need for improvements to the School buildings, drawing attention to what Allen described as 'the maze of confusing corridors, dark corners, small and dingy classrooms and the lack of resources in areas such as the Library and ICT'.

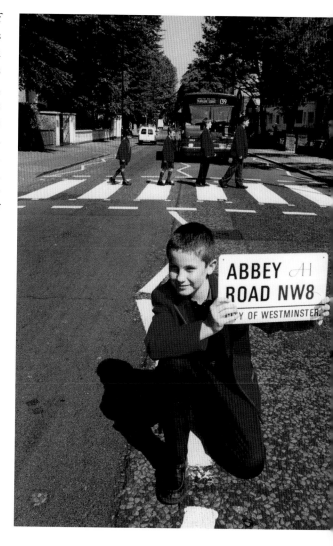

The report stimulated a discussion among the governors about a future building programme and the method of financing it. Alan Lipscomb had handed over the reins as chairman to Colin St Johnston in 1995. He had taken further forward the reform of the governing body. The departure of a number of the more conservative older governors enabled the board to become more professional, balanced and diverse in terms of its composition and the expertise of individual members. In 1996

Front and rear aspects of the School, 2003

Mrs Jo Hearnden, the headmistress of the Manor Prep School, Abingdon, became the first woman to join the governors. Overall numbers on the board were reduced to make business more manageable and a time limit of ten years was placed on tenure. Governors became more involved with the School, particularly through an education committee formed a few years later.

Of particular significance was the appointment of a new bursar, Geoffrey Simm, who succeeded John Allain in 1998. The lack of control previously exercised by the School over its own accounts had been a source of difficulty for many years. It was impossible for the governors – or the head for that matter – to have any grasp of the School's financial situation when interim accounts were always three months behind and subject to innumerable changes, causing often interminable discussions that were almost inevitably fruitless. Under Geoffrey Simm, the School finally took control of its accounts. This was a great step forward that not only gave the

governors the confidence to plan ahead but also helped to attract some outstanding candidates for future vacancies on the board.

Stemming from this, the governors agreed that a building programme could be financed by further increasing the number of boys in the School in combination with limited borrowing, increased fees and another appeal. Looking to the future, the board agreed to set aside from the additional income generated by more boys an annual sum for funding future investment in the School. Numbers were raised to 256 by increasing the average size of each form entering the School in Year 1 to 18 boys. Agreement was reached once again with the School's landlords, the Eyre Estate, about increase in rent liable from more building, and the leases on the existing buildings were renewed. The governors commissioned a study to discover the extent to which the existing site had further potential for expansion, which was followed up by a site development plan. Planning permission was

Above: Geoffrey Simm, bursar 1998–2008

achieved in the autumn of 1998 and building began in 1999. In the summer of that year Allen told the governors that 'part of the vision of the building development was to achieve a school with a real sense of unity'. By the time it was completed in 2001 at a cost of nearly £3.5 million the programme had furnished Arnold House with five new classrooms, a music suite, the George Smart Library (located in the finest room on the ground floor of No. 1, Loudoun Road), a new senior changing room, new offices, a staff work room, a larger IT room, better teaching facilities, a landscaped and unified frontage, and greater security which included a securely fenced playground.

The IT room, 2003

All the fundraising for the biggest building programme in the School's history was managed by the Headmaster. He took advantage of a travel scholarship awarded by the IAPS/English Speaking Union to study fundraising methods applied in the private education sector in the USA. This was an era when every independent UK school was beginning to take an interest in marketing as schools became more competitive. The Arnold House appeal was marketed as a centenary appeal and the first development officer, Samantha Pitcher, was appointed. She was followed by Janie Duncan and in 2002 Caroline Shepherdson became the School's first development director. An appeal committee was formed under the chairmanship of Lord Grabiner, the distinguished lawyer who was also a parent, and prospective donors were identified and approached. Many of them proved astonishingly generous. By 2001 the appeal had raised £1.25 million.

Like all major development projects, things did not always run smoothly. Relations between the various parties were strained from time to time. Then there were the unexpected setbacks. There were, for example, two floods. The roof of the gym had to be removed in preparation for the addition of another floor, and was covered over with plastic sheeting with one small corner drain. The worst storm of the summer took place one weekend in August 1999, when the School was deserted. The drain became blocked and the plastic sheeting began to sag under the weight of water, eventually giving way, with the water cascading onto the sprung floor of the gym, which was utterly ruined. The second flood occurred when the gardener watering plants in the art room found his water supply cut off at the tap – but he forgot to turn off the tap. When the supply was restored, water flowed unceasingly from half past four in the afternoon until nine the following morning, bringing down all the ceilings and pouring down the inside of the cavity walls, turning the building into a steaming sauna for several months as the water evaporated.

The gym was refurbished and reoccupied by the end of 1999. By the following spring the School was using the three new classrooms over the science laboratory, the two converted from the changing room and the two above the gym. During the course of the next year the remaining work was completed, including a new music suite and classrooms, a modernised kitchen and dining room, a new library, an IT suite and relocated offices. In the new classrooms interactive whiteboards were installed, thanks to sponsorship from a generous parent.

Canons Park
blueprint, 2000

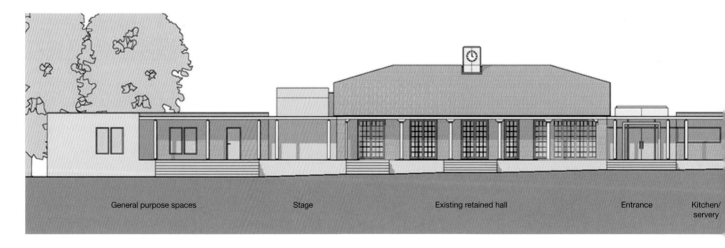

General purpose spaces   Stage   Existing retained hall   Entrance   Kitchen/servery

Year 2 in 2002, wearing the new green polo shirts

Ageing Acorn computers were replaced in 1998 with the first network of personal computers. For the George Smart Library, an experienced librarian, Leonie Flynn, was appointed. In essence she created the library from scratch, and the quality of her work at Arnold House attracted interest from other schools. Dining arrangements were subsequently improved with the introduction of a cafeteria system in 2004, helping to reduce the volume of sound made by noisy small boys and creating more space in what was still a confined area.

At the same time further work was being planned at Canons Park. A master plan was drawn up for implementation in phases over several years. The first phase envisaged a unified wing to replace the existing changing rooms, entrance lobby and tractor shed, providing two large changing rooms, a large foyer and a new kitchen. During the second phase the hall would be refurbished to create a small theatre, with a stage, lighting and retractable seating. The third phase would deliver rebuilt accommodation for the groundsman. Planning permission was granted for the scheme in 2004.

In less than a decade the School had been physically transformed. As Allen later observed, 'Having good facilities attracts good teachers and creates an atmosphere conducive to learning'. No longer could the Loudoun Road site be described as a warren of small corridors. The building programme had created a lighter, brighter and more open set of buildings that were a pleasure to work in. Canons Park provided the School with sports facilities far better than it had ever enjoyed and had given the School the space for performing arts that Loudoun Road lacked.

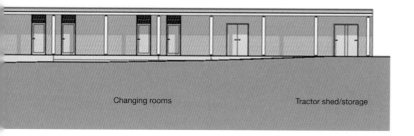

Changing rooms Tractor shed/storage

Jazz ensemble, 2002. John Linnett, Luke Birch, George Hicks and Ivo Cunningham

This contributed to the better balance that the Headmaster wanted to create between sport and the arts. He was particularly eager to give a boost to music. Teresa Burman, who had done such good work in often trying circumstances, retired as head of music in 1995. Sadly she died just a year later. Popularly known as 'Tigger', she is remembered fondly for her even temper and the relaxed nature of her lessons. George Lester paid tribute to her in the School magazine, writing that, 'Behind those sharp beady eyes and unruly hair was a very able and astute mind. She was a wise and clever bird and many valued her wisdom. Always wholehearted and generous towards her pupils, Teresa brought a great deal of enthusiasm to all she did.' Her successor, Kate Davies, also recognised Teresa Burman's achievements, writing in 2009 that she 'was a superb musician and teacher [who] laid all of the foundations for making the music department what it is today'.

Davies had arrived when the music department was still housed in the hut in the playground and teaching was often done during break:

> The front of the hut was used as a football goal and lessons would be frequently interrupted by balls flying into the side of the hut and making it shake! On very warm days, when it was necessary to teach with the door open, balls would fly in, often hitting an unsuspecting boy (or me) on the head.

She made an immediate impact on music, even though it would be five years before the department moved into its new accommodation. Musical activity grew significantly, particularly instrumental music. 'It grew and grew,' recalled Andrew Cuthbertson, 'in the most wonderful way.' The number of formal and informal concerts multiplied, with more musical productions and more visits to concerts.

Kate Davies, who was also a keen gymnast, established a harmonious relationship with the head of PE and games, Rick Martin, when she offered to help with coaching only if he agreed to play his cornet in the revived jazz band. Gymnastics was becoming one of the School's strengths. Sports organisation was steadily strengthened, leading ultimately to the appointment of Martin as director of sport, with Chris Kerr as head of games, a team of several staff and a number of specialist coaches. The scope of sport was extensive, with several School teams involved in many sports. The first under-eight football fixture, for instance, took place against Tower House, Roehampton, on 26 September 1996. Among the School's cricket stars were James Martin, who scored more than 500 runs during the 1995 season and James Japhet, whose gentle spin took 35 wickets during the 1997 season, including seven for 14 against The Hall.

Music, drama and athleticism came together in another innovation. On the evening of 27 June 1996 the first 'Fête Champêtre' took place, an event described in the School magazine as 'a celebration of music, drama, recitation and gymnastics, presented out of doors at Canons Park'. For several years this was a regular part of the School calendar but it often battled against the elements and had to be held indoors.

The Fête was one of the many occasions that brought parents into closer contact with the School. Nicholas Allen formalised the strong relationships Johnny Clegg had developed with parents and friends of the School. A weekly newsletter, *In-House*, was launched. The Friends of Arnold House was formed in 1999 primarily as a parents' association with a focus for social and educational events. The Friends, for instance, arranged auctions and appeals to raise funds for the School and for charity, organised the sale of second-hand clothing, and developed a parental involvement programme in association with the School. In 2004 another initiative, Grandparents' Day, successfully brought families closer to the School. All this sustained a generally happy relationship between parents and the School, especially since the head and his staff maintained an open-door policy.

Alongside so much change, new traditions were created, and all this strengthened the essential characteristics of the School. John Hill had been appointed head of history in 1999. He took an interest in the history of the School and was struck by the School's war memorial in St Cyprian's Church. Links between the School and the church, which had faded during Johnny Clegg's time, were revived through John Hill, whose research into boys who had died during the First World War led to the idea of taking the boys to St Cyprian's to lay a wreath at the memorial in commemoration of the Armistice. In 2001 the boys heard an address from a parent, Sebastian Faulks, whose book *Birdsong* was set in the First World War. Freddie Fox, who left the School in 2002, remembered how the boys trooped down to the church, 'like wandering poppies' in their red blazers.

The pattern of School life could seem largely unchanged, an alternating sequence of the routine and the special. Nicholas Allen's report to the governors covering the Autumn term for 1999 was typical not only in indicating the breadth of activities but also in conjuring up something of the busyness of School life.

The pace of life has continued unabated this term. Musicians have continued to rehearse; all the boys have been doing ceramics in art; teams have continued to compete against other schools; lessons have been planned and taught and special events and outings have occurred with their usual frequency. Year 8 spent an excellent week in France; there have been numerous expeditions to museums and places of interest and the term is moving towards its climax with

Musical theatre

Music became much more ambitious in the 1990s. This was epitomised in 1998 with the production of a new musical, written by the award-winning composer Denis King, who had worked with the School before, and the well-known comedy writer and lyricist Dick Vosburgh. *Upsidedownia*, co-directed by Astrid King and Kate Davies, involved staff, boys and parents. The design was based on work by Matisse and created by senior boys under the direction of Lesley Ralphs. The cast consisted of two adults (one being Nicholas Allen) and 50 boys. It was staged at the Cockpit Theatre in nearby Lisson Grove in March 1998 and was an outstanding success. Freddie Fox, who has since become a rising star of stage and screen, was among the cast. Drama, he said, 'was great because it brought everyone together and everyone had great fun doing it'.

Upsidedownia, 1998

Above: Fathers and sons cricket match, 1996

the Junior School Christmas Concert, the Middle School Musical Robin Hood, the Senior End of Term Concert and the Carol Service.

The School retained its leading position among North London prep schools. The head had written in 2000 that 'my feeling is that the comparative scarcity of places at Arnold House, combined with our broad curriculum, warm atmosphere and academic success achieved without undue pressure, give us a commanding place in the North West London market place'. The School acknowledged the need to make sure that boys were equipped to pass Common Entrance. As the Headmaster pointed out to governors in 2000, 'The School's curriculum is necessarily determined by the needs of senior schools and the need to inculcate pupils with the basic stepping stones of literacy and numeracy'. Allen was critical, as his predecessor had been, of the academic coaching some parents arranged for their sons outside School, which he regarded as unnecessary and sometimes deleterious. He was equally clear that any focus on Common Entrance should not be at

the expense of widening the boys' horizons. An inspection in 2003 had praised the School's academic standards and quality of teaching and noted that boys made good progress throughout the School, particularly in English, maths and science. But it had noted, just like other reports across the decades, that the School could provide greater opportunities for the boys to learn independently and use their initiative. It was in response to this criticism that the curriculum was broadened specifically for boys half-way through their time at Arnold House, after they had completed their grounding in learning in their early years and before their studies became concentrated upon Common Entrance. This was achieved through the medium of the Compass Course, an established method of helping boys to work both together and on their own, developing valuable skills while enhancing their own knowledge through the exploration of a range of cross-curricular topics. The course was still part of the curriculum in 2013.

Common Entrance remained a daunting prospect for many boys, as Alex Devoto outlined for the

School magazine in 1995 – 'The gym turns from a once-happy place to a room filled with distraught minds, the atmosphere speaking dread in no uncertain terms. The silence is all too loud. Eight years' work distilled into one short hour.' Arnold House boys continued to win selection to the leading public schools. In 1999, for instance, one-third of leavers had taken up places at just four schools, Eton and Winchester for those seeking boarding, Westminster and St Paul's for those wanting a day school. Scholarships continued to be achieved. In 2004 boys won scholarships to Eton, Westminster, Harrow and Mill Hill. It was unsurprising that places at Arnold House remained oversubscribed.

While Nicholas Allen undoubtedly had the vision which took Arnold House so much further forward, just as Johnny Clegg had done in his time, he also ensured he developed a strong team to support him as deputy heads or section heads. John Prosser made a valued contribution as deputy head

before his retirement in 2000 when, as Allen reported to the governors, he left the School 'bathed in the affection and respect of all who work with him'. Two deputy heads were appointed to replace him, one with responsibility for academic affairs, the other for pastoral care. The former post was assumed by Andrew Reid, who had joined the staff in 1994 and been appointed director of studies in 1995. He would leave 13 years later to become headmaster of Lyndhurst House. The second post was filled by a member of staff who had first come to Arnold House for a term's supply teaching in 1987, returning nine years later to teach full-time. This was Viv Thomas, who would also leave for a headship, at Keble School, Winchmore Hill, in 2001. Allen was also supported by people like Chere Hunter as head of the junior school, Jon Gray, who became head of middle school and later director of activities, and Rick Martin, who was appointed deputy head alongside Andrew Reid in 2003.

Year 8 Activities Week to Cumbria, early 2000s

With many staff in their 20s and 30s, the common room was full of energy and enthusiasm. John Hill recalled the great sense of camaraderie, with many staff meeting up for a drink after work several nights a week. For Nicholas Allen, what impressed him as much as anything about his colleagues was their willingness to assume responsibilities outside the classroom and demonstrate the extent of their capabilities.

For Freddie Fox, Arnold House was 'a microcosmic preparation for the rest of your life'. It not only gave boys friendship, it taught them the value of friendship. It was a safe place for young boys where they could work hard and become acquainted for the first time with the pleasures of art, music, drama and sport. 'I was very happy.' Nicky Huish, leaving the School after 20 years in 2002, reflected that 'I don't think I have ever met anyone with links

Under-ten cricket team coached by Andrew Reid, with James Japhet as captain, 1995

to Arnold House who has not left part of their heart behind'. Chere Hunter stepped down as head of the junior school in 2005. Looking back on her 28-year service, she said, 'I lived and breathed Arnold House and it was hard to leave; this was where my heart was'. Lesley Ralphs retired in 2003 after 26 years as head of art. 'Arnold House', she said, 'is quite a place, it is quite exceptional. I stayed so long because I loved it so much. I have never loved teaching as much as teaching there.'

Arnold House boy with the School flower – the red carnation. Drawing designed by Brian Byfield, 2004

Year 2 boys in the
refurbished Music
Suite, 2012

7

'Happy Boys Will Learn'
2005 onwards

In 2005 Arnold House celebrated its centenary.
Two years previously the Centenary Path had
been launched with old boys and current pupils
sponsoring individual bricks along the forecourt
at the front of the School. During the centenary
year itself a ball was held at the Dorchester for staff,
parents and friends in March. In May the boys
enjoyed a special tea party and a celebratory concert
was held in St John's Wood Church. The '42
Club dinner that year took place in the Tallow
Chandlers' Hall. On 29 September, St Michael's
Day, a special service was arranged, followed by an
evening cocktail party.

In celebrating the centenary, and looking back
at the achievements of previous heads, Nicholas
Allen could also be proud of his own contribution
to the School. His organisational strengths had
helped to bring the School up to date. It had
become a modern school in the way in which it was
run from day to day inside and outside the
classroom and in the scope of its buildings and
facilities. He had been outstanding in raising funds

The School arms

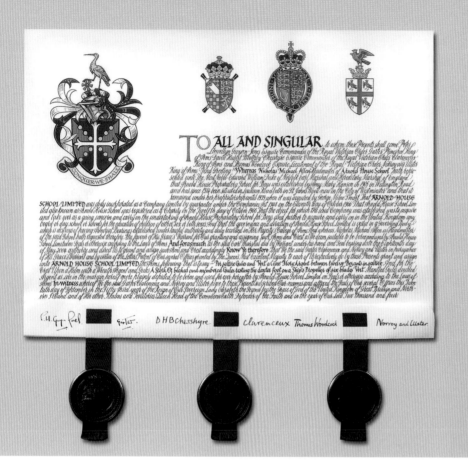

In 2004 the School applied for a grant of arms. The design made reference to all four houses, Nelson, Pitt, Wellington and Brunel, and to Miss Hanson, with red and green as background colours, and using a shortened form – 'Conquer We Shall' – of the motto adopted by the founder. The silver cross at the centre of the shield alludes to the arms of Lord Nelson and to Miss Hanson's devout Christian faith. The gold discs around the cross refer to the arms of the Duke of Wellington. The crest is formed of a stork, which refers to the arms of Pitt the Younger, while the propeller on which the stork rests its foot refers to the great engineer Isambard Kingdom Brunel.

to finance these developments and had been an excellent public ambassador for the School. Allen could be very supportive of his staff; Annabel Batty, who arrived at Arnold House in 1997, later observed that 'if you went to him for advice, he always got it right'.

By 2005 for a variety of reasons both the Headmaster and the governors were seeking a change. Allen was conscious that he should not outstay his welcome and wanted another challenge before retirement. The governors were very clear about the qualities they sought from a new head. They wanted one who might combine the overt warmth of Johnny Clegg with the organisational skills of his successor. Allen was appointed as headmaster of a relatively young school, Newton Prep, on the south side of the river, taking over in 2006. A few years later his peers would recognise his

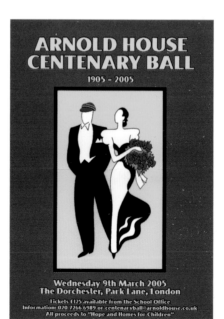

Centenary celebrations: a poster and ticket for the ball and, opposite, the centenary cake, with, standing left: Alfie Murray, Jacob Dicker, Zac Cutner, Caroline Shepherdson; standing right: Toby Green, James Green; kneeling: Angelo Lemos, Yannis Lemos, Charlie Green and Yiannis Fafalios

Viv Thomas with Mo Mussa, Joel Sharpe and William Evans, 2010

contribution to the prep-school movement by electing him as chairman of IAPS, representing the headteachers of leading prep schools both in the UK and abroad.

The appointment of Allen's successor was announced in June 2005. The governors, under a new chairman, former parent Alan Warner, had turned for the next Headmaster of Arnold House to someone who already knew the School very well. This was Viv Thomas, who had left the School in 2001 to take up his first headship. He was educated at University College School, Hampstead, after which he trained to be a teacher at St Luke's College, Exeter University where he represented the university 1st teams in three sports; rugby, football and tennis. After five years' teaching in London prep schools (including a short spell at Arnold House in the summer term of 1987) he took up a post at his old senior school teaching PE and maths and within three years was promoted to director of sport. Thomas was prompted to further his career elsewhere on being described by one of the masters who had taught him as 'a lifer'. Having married, he and his wife Rowena spent two years in Venezuela where he taught maths at the American International School of Caracas. He returned to the UK and was recruited by Nicholas Allen as head of maths at Arnold House. He quickly became senior master and then deputy head before leaving to run Keble School. He had been sorry to leave Arnold House, having greatly enjoyed the academic, sporting and pastoral aspects of his role within the School. He had no hesitation in applying for the headship when it came up four years later. He had learned a great deal from his time at Keble and he particularly enjoyed supporting and guiding good staff. Both Arnold House and Keble had given him an appreciation of the value of boys' prep schools, their spirit and sense of fun.

Viv Thomas came back to Arnold House in September 2006. In his own words, Arnold House was 'a cracking school to take on'. The work done by Nicholas Allen had established a sound organisation, delivering a broad education through excellent staff, enabling boys to move on to the most sought-after senior schools in the country. His return was marked by less apprehension than might have been the case with a complete newcomer. Many of the staff knew him, and his appointment was widely welcomed. The governors were confident that he understood and valued the School ethos. This came through clearly at the first address the new Headmaster made at Prize Giving. He took as his theme 'Happy Boys Will Learn', a constant part of the School's philosophy since its foundation. He outlined how that might be sustained in a modern boys' prep school in the 21st century. Firstly, by making boys feel safe and valued. Arnold House had the virtues of a small school, with 250 boys in eight year groups, and a pupil–teacher ratio of 9:1. This, Thomas believed, was an ideal size, 'allowing room for healthy competition without being overwhelming'. (Miss Hanson would have been delighted to hear that a century on the person leading Arnold House was as adamant as she had been that teaching in small groups helped to reinforce good manners, courtesy and the right approach to studying.) Secondly, by keeping boys busy with varied activities, of which the School had an impressive range. And, thirdly,

by encouraging boys to aim high and always do their best, borne out by the most recent examination results. Of 230 Scholarship and Common Entrance papers taken in English, Mathematics, Biology, Chemistry, Physics, French, Latin, Greek, History, Geography and Religious Studies in 2007, 86 per cent achieved grades A or B and 59 per cent grade A, a pattern that has remained relatively constant. Several exhibitions and scholarships had been awarded and that year boys had won places at Bryanston, Charterhouse, Eton, Harrow, Highgate, Lancing, Latymer Upper, Mill Hill, St Paul's, Westminster, Winchester and UCS.

Boys were also taking part in history, literary and art and design competitions. In 2008 Jonah Mendelsohn became national champion in the Townsend-Warner History Prize competition while a team consisting of Alec Badenoch, Louis Cross, Hugo Darwood and Rishabh Watts became world champions in the Kids' Lit Quiz. Arnold House, Thomas had written in the School magazine for June 2007, offered 'an exceptionally warm and purposeful environment in which young boys can learn and mature at their own pace'. Thomas was especially keen to emphasise the all-round nature of the education offered by the School and to sustain its high quality. He particularly wanted to develop a greater focus on each boy as an individual whether inside or outside the classroom. More specialist subject teachers and teaching assistants were appointed and in the classroom there was more emphasis on ensuring every boy was taught at the level appropriate for his abilities. Most recently an academic committee, comprising the head, deputy head, director of studies, heads of department and head of learning support, was established to formalise the way the progress of individual boys was tracked.

Left: a plaque to commemorate the Townsend-Warner History Prize, 2008

Right: Kids' Lit Quiz world champions.
Back row: The Mayor of Oxford and Professor Wayne Mills.
Front row: Hugo Darwood, Louis Cross, Rishabh Watts and Alec Badenoch

Below: Summer Concert at Canons Park with director of music Paul Swinden, 2010

It was important, Thomas believed, to appreciate the achievements of every boy. No longer would prizes in the first year be limited to just 'First Boy' and 'Second Boy'; every boy in the pre-prep would gain confidence from the public acknowledgement of his achievement. While Headmaster's certificates and standards reports were introduced to help give boys a clearer understanding of what was expected from them, the scope of the rewards system was widened to recognise industry as much as high academic merit. In School reports more emphasis was placed on the overall contribution of each boy, with the introduction of a citizenship report that formally recognised a boy's conduct in class, courtesy around School and wider contribution to School life through music and the arts, sports, clubs, activities and responsibilities. There was a need to instil this awareness more widely

within the staff. When the only forum for every member of staff was the formal staff meeting, it was tempting to concentrate solely on the academic side of the School. To involve the staff more widely in the breadth of the education offered by the School Thomas initiated a sports festival that took place once a term on a Saturday morning at Canons Park which all staff were expected to attend. Similarly, every member of staff, including the Headmaster, was expected to lead an activity for the boys. Thomas himself, with his interest in maths, led a darts club.

Thomas knew that part of the character of Arnold House was its respect for the past but he also believed that an equally intrinsic part of its nature was that it was 'a school which lives in the moment'. Innovative changes were made to the curriculum. For instance, drama was added to the timetable for Years 3–6, the science department ran a Science Week, the history department a History Week, and a course in music technology was introduced for boys in Year 8.

Above: Science Week with Year 7 Louis Cutner and Shaan Kotecha

Left: Music Composition with Antonio Tarizzo and Sam Hodder-Williams

Cellists Sacha
McDonell, Ayomide
Soleye, Daniyal
Sachee and Charlie
Lewis

Learning support was expanded, helping boys to make progress more swiftly, with a team of teaching assistants, a specialist support teacher and a visiting speech and language therapist. iMacs were acquired for the music department and netbooks made available for boys in classrooms to access the internet.

In music Kate Davies and her team, including talented peripatetic teachers drawn from the colleges of music, were achieving remarkable levels of participation. In 2007 at least 80 per cent of boys in Years 3–8 were learning at least one instrument. In 2011 the recently appointed director of music, Paul Swinden, and his newly formed chapel choir performed for the first time in the chapel of the Hospital of St John and St Elizabeth. Under Kate Housden, the art syllabus was broadened to encompass art, craft and design, bringing in felt making, textiles and print making. One collaboration with the science department led the boys to create slides of their skin and cheek cells, as well as exploring the structures of crystals, all of which

became the basis for imaginative textile work and painting exhibited to the rest of the School. Drama received a boost with the appointment of the first head of drama, David Moss-Marks. Years 3–4 held their own annual arts festival and Years 5–7 had their own drama clubs. Drama Days were offered, a house drama competition was launched and Year 8 boys were given the opportunity to take part in the Shakespeare Schools Festival, to which Moss-Marks brought Arnold House for the first time in the autumn of 2009. He recalled how, as a novice director, he found that 'the build-up was frantic, never having taken on such a task before, and there were a few hair-raising moments'. The show itself was particularly memorable for one boy giving his all as Lady Macbeth, dressed in a gold lamé outfit made by one of the parents.

The choise of activities on offer would have amazed boys of earlier generations. Seb Stones had been appointed director of activities by Nicholas Allen and the programme was given fresh impetus by Thomas's belief that as many teachers, support staff and boys should participate as possible. Under Seb Stones and his successor David Cox, dozens

Above: End of Term Service at St John's Wood Church, 2010

Left: Year 8 boys performing in *Much Ado about Nothing* at the Platform Theatre, Shakespeare Schools Festival, 2012

more activities sprung up. In the summer of 2013, for instance, 61 sessions of clubs, activities and music groups were listed in the School calendar ranging from ju-jitsu and short tennis to cookery and George Lester's long-established heraldic art club. As Seb Stones observed, 'There's something for everybody, not just for the sporty boys who enjoy football or cricket, but also for boys who like stamp-collecting or drama. There are few prep schools with so much to offer.'

The library

The library had become a central part of school life. In 2010 Leonie Flynn wrote that 'There are few things more delightful than seeing a child glowing with enthusiasm over a just-finished book. It is even better when they share that excitement with their peers'. One boy, Jonah Freud, who was head librarian, lamented in the same year that 'Of all the things at Arnold House the library is the one I am going to miss the most'. A more extensive programme of visiting speakers covered topics including working with the homeless, safety on the internet, the work of the local hospice, the building of the Shard, environmental issues and, in a talk by one of his descendants, the life of Captain Smith of the *Titanic*.

Visits and excursions were almost innumerable: a Monet exhibition, the *Golden Hind*, the Globe Theatre, the Cirque du Soleil. The First World War battlefields in France and Belgium became a regular

Left: Year 5
Teambuilding
week in Devon,
2011

Below: Canons
Park Activity
Centre, 2010

destination for senior boys. They were guided by a specialist and discovered more about former pupils of the School who had died on active service. This was part of a more coherent programme of residential trips, which in 2011 also included separate weeks in Devon for boys in Year 5 and Year 6, learning about teamwork and leadership respectively, an art and French trip to Paris for boys in Year 7, and a French immersion week in Burgundy for boys in Year 8. Rachel Ferhaoui who led more than 50 trips abroad, mainly to France, bore witness to a fund of stories. One trip to Aigues-Mortes, she recalled, 'coincided with the annual "Let's let the angry bulls charge through the streets baited by the fearless youths of the city" Festival. Needless to say, I hadn't risk-assessed or anticipated that one, so we just made a hasty dash for the city ramparts, to keep out of harm's way!'

The development at Canons Park was completed in January 2007, and opened formally that summer.

Under the direction of Rick Martin from 2005 until 2011, the Canons Park Activity Centre, as it was now known, became an invaluable facility. It was the location for a host of events, including the termly sports festivals Viv Thomas had introduced as well as drama, music concerts and the Fête Champêtre. It was also extensively used by local groups, including the Middlesex Ladies' Cricket Association, the Primrose Hill Cricket Club, bowls and tennis clubs, the local police and various charity groups. They were attracted in part because of the high standards maintained by groundsman John Dawson from his arrival at Canons Park in 1992 until his retirement in 2007 and afterwards by his successor Paul Martin. In 2009–10 Rick Martin could write that in the School's third full year at Canons Park, 'we have found a rhythm that is governed by the needs of the school, the local community and the weather'.

Similarly boys benefited from expanded sporting opportunities devised by Chris Kerr, now director of sport, and his team. With the introduction of games afternoons for two year groups at a time, it was

Above: Rugby at Canons Park, 2010

Left: Football Festival, 2011

possible to offer higher-quality coaching and relieve pressure on facilities that could become crowded. In 2007 School cricket teams played nearly 50 matches, with the 1st XI winning all except one of their matches. By 2008, for football, cricket, rugby, hockey and tennis, there were teams for all ability levels so that every boy had an opportunity to represent the School. The use of additional facilities at Paddington Recreation Ground, Seymour Leisure Centre and Swiss Cottage Leisure Centre allowed boys to enjoy rock climbing, badminton, tennis, cricket nets and athletics during PE lessons. By increasing the number of tennis courts at Canons Park to six in 2008, it was possible for two hockey matches to be played simultaneously on the extended all-weather surface. More

Above: Twenty/20 cricket at Lord's, 2009, and, left, the Memorial Challenge Cup

The Art Room
with Head of Art,
Kate Housden,
2010

ambitious cricket tours were organised, to the West of England in 2007 and Jersey in 2008. This was also the year of the first Twenty/20 fixture held at Lord's in memory of Johnny Clegg, who had died in 2006, and John Allain, the former bursar, who had died in 2007, both lovers of the game. Chris Kerr summed up the approach at Arnold House thus: 'It is always a great pleasure to watch boys in Year 1 trying to master the basics of running, jumping and catching, transform into young men playing a whole range of sports with great skill and in the spirit of good sportsmanship. Hopefully this foundation, developed at Arnold House, will remain with the boys long after they have grown out of their red blazers.'

The Headmaster and the Board of Friends
invite you to attend the Arnold House

BURSARY FUND
GALA

THURSDAY 12TH MAY 2011,
19:30

The American School in London

The evening will include;
A THREE COURSE GALA DINNER, DRINKS &
AN AUCTION OF PROMISES CONDUCTED BY
LORD DALMENY, DEPUTY CHAIRMAN, SOTHEBY'S UK.

£55 PER PERSON

In aid of the Bursary Fund.

Please contact Stephanie Miller at
smiller@arnoldhouse.co.uk
or phone 020 7266 6989 to purchase tickets.

ARNOLD HOUSE SCHOOL

Viv Thomas continued the process of modern-
ising the management of the School. In 2008
Geoffrey Simm retired as bursar and Richard
Fletcher, with a career in commercial banking,
was appointed as his successor. He, along with
newly appointed deputy heads, John Hill and
Seb Stones, met with Thomas regularly as a
Strategy Team. It was here, for example, that with
ingenious planning it was made possible to
squeeze even more out of the Loudoun Road site
with the creation of four new teaching rooms in
the attic of No. 3 in 2011. Always appreciative of
the work of the staff, Thomas was also happy to

Richard Fletcher,
bursar since 2009

Right: Jacob Caroll using a microscope purchased through the 2012 Annual Fund

Below: Annual Fund leaflet, 2012

The Annual Fund 2012

The Annual Fund 2011 was very successful and each item has now been purchased or is in the process of being purchased. Donations to the Annual Fund allow the School to immediately finance projects and items, which directly enhances the facilities available for teaching and learning. More recently, these items have included the purchase of an A3 printing press for the Art & Design department, an LCD Touch Screen for the Pre-Prep, video recorders for the Science department and keyboards for the Music department.

The School is most grateful to those parents and old boys who have supported these projects.

The Annual Fund 2012 again represents a selection of small and immediate projects for the benefit of current pupils.

If you would like to purchase one or part of one of the items listed on the right hand side, please contact Stephanie Miller, Director of Development, on 020 7266 6989 or at smiller@arnoldhouse.co.uk. Alternatively please complete the form on the back of this leaflet and return it to Arnold House School, 1 Loudoun Road, St. John's Wood, London, NW8 0LH.

Thank you in advance for your support.

Items for the Annual Fund 2012
(approximate cost is given in brackets)

Drama
- Commedia Dell'Arte Masks (£450)

Music
- Replacement Drum Kit (£500)

Recording Studio
- 1 Macbook Pro to run recording software Logic 9 (£1500)
- Logic 9 software (£140)
- MOTU 8 Pre-device connecting 8 microphones to a virtual/studio mixer (£400)
- Microphones (£500)
- Microphone stands, leads and wires (£250)
- 8-way multicore – to send audio signals to the mixer (£58)

Library
- Kindles x 10 (£89 each)
- Kindle covers x 10 (£20 each)

Science
- Student 5kS2 Microscopes x 10 (£125 each)
- Advanced Digital Microscope x 1 (£380)

Sports
- Table tennis tables x2 (£300 each)
- Mini tennis net for indoor use (£100)
- Cricket Score Board (£1500)
- Winmau Dartboard cabinets x2 (£35 each)

delegate while retaining a watching brief. Responsibility for day-to-day running of the School was given to a management team. By 2012 this consisted of the two deputy heads, the heads of year Chris Kerr, Lizzie Jones and Susie Dart and the director of studies, Rekha Ruda. Heads of year was an innovation Thomas took from his experience at UCS and they helped to underpin the pastoral care provided by form teachers. The management team met weekly and on more than one occasion Thomas recalled '... exercised excellent judgement in resisting change for change's sake'.

Thomas and his staff fostered warm relations with parents. An Open House was introduced for current parents, and termly social events were arranged for the parents and staff of each year group. The Friends of Arnold House had been superseded by a more conventional Parents' Association, which carried on similar work, including fundraising for furnishing the School and assisting staff with travel grants as well as for charities. The Association was responsible for organising the annual disco for Years 6–8, described by the Association's chair in 2010 as 'famous in the girls' schools of North London'. The attitude of the boys had clearly changed since earlier days, as parent Gabrielle Sharpe noted, 'It is always amazing to see the metamorphosis of our boys before our very eyes – teeth brushed, hair combed and even shoes cleaned! The boys talk of nothing else in the lead up to the event and spend the week afterwards comparing how many phone numbers they have managed to collect!'

Fundraising was developing into a more streamlined sphere of the School's activities. The role of the development office continued to evolve. A development committee was formed which eventually became the Board of Friends in 2009, chaired by former pupil Anastassis Fafalios. The Board played a key role in launching the School's Bursary Fund, financed partly by gifts and sponsorship and partly by the School surplus. The Fund stemmed from the notion of public benefit that the Charity Commission linked with the continuance of the charitable status of independent schools, although Arnold House, thanks originally to Miss Hanson, had been making small awards for many years. The disadvantage for Arnold House lay in the uncertainty that any bursary holder would achieve a place in senior public schools. Alan Warner, who became chairman of governors in 2003, knew that his old school, Rugby, was assessing able boys from modest backgrounds for admission, and an agreement was reached that Arnold House would educate such a boy for two years prior to his taking up a place at Rugby. Ken Durham, the headmaster of UCS and a member of the governing body, gave advice on the best way to recruit deserving boys from the local area. As a result of all this planning, the first bursary pupil was admitted in 2007. Two more bursaries were awarded in September 2009 and this number continued to increase, with four offered in September 2011. In the first four years more than £250,000 was raised for the Fund and Mill Hill became another destination senior school for bursary boys. At the

The School's birthday tradition – Year 8 versus the staff tug-of-war, September 2012

same time what was called the Annual Fund was established to help pay for items directly linked to teaching and learning. In 2010, for instance, this raised £24,000 to fund improvements to music, sport, computing and the library.

Among the boys, fundraising was also becoming a more organised activity. In 2007 a charity committee was established, made up of a member of staff and three older boys, focused on helping local and national charities. As well as raising money through a variety of events, boys also learned about the work of different charities across the world, often from specially invited speakers. In 2010, for example, boys raised almost £14,000 for charities. This was linked with the School's unchanged religious approach, summed up by John Hill in 2009, when he said that the School celebrated 'its Christian ethos whilst being sensitive to other religious traditions'. In 2006 at the suggestion of Hill, who had initiated the ceremony

of laying the wreath at the war memorial, the School revived the tradition of celebrating St Michael's Day on 29 September as the first service of the School year. The School's birthday is now accompanied by a series of recent traditions, including a tug of war between staff and Year 8 boys, the cutting of a cake and, in the evening, a reception for staff and old boys.

The improvements achieved under Viv Thomas and his staff made a strong impression on the Independent Schools Inspectorate during their visit to Arnold House in February 2009. One word – 'outstanding' – peppered the inspectorate's conclusions. The School offered a strong education with outstanding features, characterised by good quality and often outstanding teaching, with an outstanding extra-curricular programme and outstanding links with parents and the local community. As for the boys, noted the report, 'By the time the pupils reach their transfer point at the

Cutting the School's 106th birthday cake in 2011

age of 13, they are articulate, confident and converse easily with adults and their peers ... The relationships between the staff and pupils are excellent'. As John Hill observed, Arnold House remained a place where there was as much emphasis on friendship as on hard work. Viv Thomas had written in 2008 how 'It has always been the Arnold House way to educate boys in the broadest sense and to equip them with the social graces, confidence and well-roundedness to enable them to flourish at their chosen senior schools'. It was, said Annabel Batty, a warm, welcoming and compassionate place for both boys and staff. 'There isn't a place like it. The children are so happy here. The boys look out for each other and the staff look out for the boys and look after each other.' One former pupil, now a parent, reflected on how the School had brought out the best in his sons, offering them an all-round education, encouraging competition and hard work, helping them to see things in the round as a foundation for their future. Susie Dart, head of the pre-prep, pointed to three boys from the same family, all with very different personalities, each one of whom loved being at the School. Arnold House, she observed, was small enough to nurture boys for their individuality, whether academic, athletic, artistic or eccentric. This was a point borne out by one teacher, David Cox, who remembered a football match where a boy was standing in defence while an opposing player ran at him towards the goal with the ball. Rather than make an attempt at a challenge he stood utterly still and let his opponent go past. The boy was asked, 'Why didn't you make an attempt to tackle him?' 'I was thinking, sir', replied the boy. 'What do you mean you were thinking?' 'I was thinking about the French Revolution, sir.' David Cox did not recall being able to come up with a meaningful response!

Arnold House owes much to Amy Hanson. The remarkable thing about the School is that however much the fabric might have changed, or the mode of teaching, or the content of the curriculum, or almost any other aspect of the School, the one thing that remains the same today as it did in 1905 is its character. Somehow this has been handed down and nurtured not just by successive heads but also by successive generations of teachers and boys. The cosmopolitan nature of the neighbourhood in which Amy Hanson set Arnold House may have something to do with it, fostering the tolerance that is so much a part of the School. A look back at the first years of the School reveals that those things that staff, parents and pupils value most were all set down by the founder. She valued each boy for what he was. She wanted each boy to develop his own potential to the full without placing him under undue pressure. She encouraged boys to do their best, to be honourable and self-reliant. She encouraged them to consider those less fortunate than themselves. She wanted them to cherish the past while looking to the future. She fostered in many of them a deep loyalty to the School stemming from the close personal interest she took in their lives once they left Arnold House.

She also chose her successor well, as Arnold House owes just as much to George Smart. A very different personality, who exuded a greater warmth than his predecessor, he nevertheless shared everything she stood for. His life, just like hers, was based upon Arnold House. He invested in the School so much more than he took out. He took it through the difficult days of the Second World War and secured its future by transferring it to a charitable trust. Through hard times and good he sustained and strengthened the characteristics of the School he had taken over.

Of those who came after him, Johnny Clegg, Nicholas Allen and Viv Thomas have all helped to guide the School through changing times, each of them making their own mark on the place, but each of them faithful to the principles on which it was founded. Many staff too, from Marguerite Hasencleaver and John Robson to Chere Hunter and George Lester, have played their part in helping to steer the School through change while cherishing its distinctive ethos.

The greatest witness to this truth may be found in the many former pupils aged from 18 to 80 and more who look back on their early education at Arnold House as more of a foundation for their later life than their days at senior school. Above all, many of them as they left Arnold House at the age of just 13 took with them friendships that have lasted the rest of their days. What better testimonial does a school need?

Arnold House School, May 2013

Index

Photo acknowledgements

The majority of the photographs in the book come from the School's archive. The School and TMI Publishing would also like to thank Nicky Colton-Milne, Roy Fox, Tony Quill and Charlotte Wood for their modern photography as well as the following individuals and organisations:

p15 (top) National Portrait Gallery, London; p16 (left) © Wellcome Library, London (right) © Mary Evans Picture Library/Arthur Rackman; p30 by kind permission of the Marx Memorial Library; p42 (middle) © British Empire and Commonwealth Museum / Cultural Heritage Images (bottom) courtesy of Peter Kemp; p53 (bottom) by kind permission of The Ryder family and The Times; p66 © The Press Association; p75 © Illustrated London News Ltd/Mary Evans; p126 (top right) © National Portrait Gallery, London; pp154–55 © Tempest Photography.

Every effort has been made to trace copyright holders and to obtain their permission for the use of copyright material. TMI Publishing apologises for any errors or omissions in the above list and would be grateful if notified of any corrections that should be incorporated in future editions of this book.